FNITEK'S LINUX
LAB
FOR
BEGINNERS

Chibueze O. Meremikwu

Table of Content

FOREWORD

Linux is a free and open-source Unix-like operating system. It was developed by the Linux community for computer frameworks, mainframes, servers, and mobile and embedded devices. Presently, you can run Linux from your web browsers. In recent years, it has come to be one of the widely accepted OS that supports virtually every large computer platform such as ARM, Linux SPARC, and x86.

Linux OS can be accessed by anyone with programming experience and it also offers access to millions of applications and software. Fnitek's Linux Labs for Beginners demystifies the understanding of Linux and breaks it into components that you can understand easily with screenshots and code snippets.

If you have been searching for a book to help you navigate the word of Linux, here is the right compass for you.

Journey with me as we navigate the world of Linux through the pages of this book.

LAB ONE

INTRODUCTION TO BASIC LINUX COMMAND

In this chapter, I will introduce the basic Linux commands.

The Basic Commands Introduced In this chapter are:

- script
- echo
- pwd
- Is
- man
- cmkdir
- touch
- Isb_release
- rm

This chapter also guides you on how to:

- Connect/Disconnect From Lab Environment
- Record What You Do With Typescript

- Determine Linux Description
- Itemize Current Working Directory Contents
- Create / Delete Files And Directories
- Change Directories
- Basic Linux File system Knowledge

UNDERSTANDING EACH COLOUR BOX

Throughout this session, you will see three different colour boxes. Each colour indicates something different. A **BLACK** box indicates a command to run. A GREEN box indicates a question that you will need to answer. A TURQUOISE box tells you what to do on your own.

An example of each follows:

A **BLACK** box will tell you what commands to run on your environment. Each black box is pre-seeded with a % sign. This sign is an example of a command prompt.

CAUTION: DO NOT TYPE THE PRE-SEEDED % SIGN!

Type only what follows with the % sign.

```
%  this _is_a_command
```

A GREEN box will indicate a question. All questions must
be answered correctly. When answering questions, you will
need to run a command called 'read'. Type out exactly what
is in a green box and then hit the <return> key. Once you
see your question printed out onto the terminal, type out
your answer. Hit the <return> key again to save your
answer. If you make a mistake or if you want to type a
different answer, just retype what is in the green box of the
question.

```
reap -p "why is the sky blue? " question [Θ]
```

A TURQUOISE box will give you a task to do on your own.

NOW YOU TRY THIS
Do 5 Push-Ups

DO NOT PROCEED UNLESS YOU GET THE FOLLOWING OUTPUT:

Script started, the file is typescript

STAGE 1 | THE SHELL / THE INTERPRETER

You probably have noticed by now that you are not working with a GUI but on a command-line interface. The command line is what you use to interact with the lab server. This interface is known as a SHELL. A SHELL is an interpreter. It interprets the commands you give it and turns it into a language that the server will understand. There are many SHELLs available that users can use. Some of these SHELLs and Interpreters include:

- KSH (**K**orn **SH**ell)
- BASH (**B**ourne **A**gain **SH**ell)
- ZSH (**Z**-**SH**ell)
- SH

To determine which SHELL you are using, you will need to read the value of 2 environment variables and relay them onto your terminal. The command to display a variable value onto your terminal is the **echo**. To achieve this, we need to read the following variables:

SHELL

0

The SHELL variable contains your default SHELL environment. This is the SHELL that will load every time you log on. The 0 variable contains the currently running process. In this case, the current running process would be your SHELL environment.

To read the contents of a variable, you need to pre-seed the variable with a $ symbol. Let's go ahead and echo the value of the SHELL variable. To do this we will call the echo command and give it the variable to be read.

```
% echo  $ SHELL
```

This will echo out your default SHELL environment. This is the environment that you should expect to use by default when logging onto the environment.

NOW YOU TRY THIS

Go ahead and output the value that is stored in the 0 variable. Use the same

STAGE 2 I LINUX & THE FILESYSTEM

So what operating system are you using? It is Linux. Linux is an open

source operating system that is based on UNIX. Linux comes in

many different flavors. The most known Linux distribution families are:

- Debian
- Arch
- RPM
- Fedora
- RHEL (Red Hat Enterprise Linux)

Each family has many distributions built off of them. The most popular are Ubuntu which is based on Debian and CentOS which is based on RHEL. Distributions can also build upon themselves within their family. For example, another popular Linux distribution is called ***Linux Mint***. Linux Mint is built off of Ubuntu which is built off of Debian.

Who Uses Linux?

Everyone can use an alternative server technology. It can be enjoyed freely or come at a cost. Some alternatives are of course Microsoft Windows and Mac OS X Server.

Linux, however, is the most popular operating system that is used on the majority of servers today. The 3 main reasons for this are:

- It's free and open-source
- It is highly secured
- It is very efficient

Linux is an open-source project. This means that you have plenty of people who are always contributing to making Linux better, faster, more reliable, and more secure. This also means that a lot more eyes are watching the code for any security vulnerability. It is expected for Linux packages to be updated frequently when compared to applications on other operating systems. This also means that Linux is free to use. Who doesn't love free things? Linux is also very efficient. Most of the server's processing power are used to process what you need it to and not process junk like fancy GUIs or inefficient code.

So what flavor of Linux is the lab environment running? Luckily there is a command for us. The ***lsb_release*** command with the -a flag will output your Linux distribution, its version, and other information. It's as simple as typing in the command to get all of this information. Go ahead and run it now and see what Linux distro you are using

```
% lsb_release -a
```

Not all environments will have this package installed so you will need to do other things to determine the Linux distro like an echo out the release file located in the etc directory.

Everything Is A File

One key thing to know about Linux is that everything is a file! Directories are also considered files. Directories are complex files that tell the interpreter how to determine what files should be stored within the "directory". A directory is an executable file. To see the contents inside of a directory it must be executable. If it isn't then you won't be able to see or change into that directory.

Linux uses a file structure known as the Filesystem Hierarchy Standard (FHS). The Linux structure begins at the root directory which is located at '/'. An image of a common mapping of the Linux File Structure is located on the next page.

Each directory in Linux serves a purpose. What is meant by this is that every directory is home to a set of files that have the same general purpose. For example, *the/home* file is home to the system user's home directory. The/home directory will contain a folder for each user that uses the system for his or her files. The/boot directory contains files that aid in the boot-up of the operating system. The/etc directory includes configuration files for the operating system and any packages installed on the system.

Getting Around

The question then is, how exactly do we get around this structure with a command line interface? With a command of course. To change the directory, we use the change directory command: **cd**

With **cd** (change directory) you can traverse the Linux directory by giving it a relative path to the directory where you wish to go, an absolute path, or use a shortcut. Once you change directories, you may want to see what files or directories are inside of that directory. To do this we use the **Is** (list) command.

Let's try changing directories to the /*usr* directory. We are going to use an absolute path to get there. We will then list the contents of this directory. An absolute path means that you are going to start from the root directory '/' and work your way from there to another directory. In this example, we are starting from the root path and going to the 'usr' directory.

```
% cd /usr
% ls
```

Now let's try changing into another directory within the /usr directory. Let's try changing into the 'local' directory. This time since we are already in the /usr directory we don't need to give the absolute path if the directory is located within the directory we are currently in. We can just give a relative path. Change the directory to the local directory by issuing the following command:

```
% cd local
```

Since we were already in the /usr directory, by giving the relative path of just 'local', the system will start at the directory you were in and traverse forward from there.

If you ever forget what directory you are in you can always use the **pwd** command to show you. The pwd command will **p**rint your current **w**orking **d**irectory in an absolute path format. Try it now to see the absolute path of the directory you are currently in:

```
% pwd
```

The change directory command also comes with a few shortcuts to make traversing the filesystem a bit easier and faster. These shortcuts are listed in the table on the right.

Currently, you should be within the 'local' directory inside of the 'usr' directory. If you want to go back to the '/usr' directory.

This can be done using either of these two ways:

- Use the absolute path to get back
- Use a shortcut to go back to one directory

CD Shortcuts

../	Goes back to one directory. Can be chained to go back x amount of times until it reaches the root directory.
~	A shortcut that changes directories back to your home directory

cd	Running the cd command on its own with no argument will also change directories back to your home directory.

Let's try using a shortcut that will get us back to the '/usr' directory. Once you run the cd command use the pwd command to verify that you went back to 1 directory.

```
% cd ../
% pwd
```

What should have been printed out is '/usr' indicating that you did go back to one directory. If you wanted to go back 2 directories from the 'local' directory, then you would have ran the cd command with ../../to take you back 2 directories. Taking you back 2 directories would have landed you back at the root directory

STAGE 3 l USING THE MANUAL PAGES

Most Linux distributions will not leave you in the dark when it comes to figuring out what a command does and what kind of options the command can take to get you a different result. Linux distributions can come prepackaged with a package known as the manual pages or man pages for short. If a distribution does not come with the man pages they can be installed. The man pages can also include examples of how to run a command.

Make sure you are in your home directory by running the pwd command. Your home directory should be similar to /home/users#/your_username

```
% pwd
```

Once you have verified that you are in your home directory go ahead and run the *ls* command to list all the contents of your directory.

```
% ls
```

You should be viewing all of the content in your home directory, right? Wrong! The list command will only list what is not hidden. Directories can contain hidden files and directories that will not be listed if you just run the list command as is. You will need to supply the list command with an option that will list all files and directories including all hidden files and directories. We will use the man pages to find this option.

To use the manual pages we will use the **man** command. Following the command is the command you wish to get more information about. In our case, we will look at the man pages for the list command. Open up the man pages and read through them. Find the option that will list all of the files, including hidden ones. Once you find the option quit the man pages by typing **q** and then run the Is command with the option you found.

```
% man ls
```

Let's look for one more option. Search the man pages for the option that will allow you to list the contents of the current directory in a long list format. Once you find the option run the command with that option.

STAGE 4 | CREATING FILES AND DIRECTORIES

The last part of this lab will cover creating some files and directories. Make sure you are in your home directory before continuing with this stage.

The first thing we will do is create a new directory called 'cit'. To create a directory we will use the make directory command: **mkdir**. Run the following command to create this directory.

```
% mkdir cit
```

Run the Is command. You should see your newly created directory. Go ahead and change into the 'cit' directory.

Only one directory can be created at a time with the mkdir command. Let's say that you need to create a 'my tasks' directory within a 'my_class' directory but the 'my_class' directory does not yet exist. To do this you will need to supply the mkdir command with the -p option. The -p option will create any needed parent directories. In this case, it will create the 'my class' directory first and then the 'my tasks' directory. Try creating the 2 directories nested within each other without the -p option. After you see the error it produced, run the command again but with the -p option. You should still be within the 'cit' directory when running these commands.

```
% mkdir my_class/my_tasks
% mkdir -p my_class/my_tasks
```

Change directories to the 'my_tasks' directory within the 'my_class' directory. We can use a relative path for this since these directories are inside of the directory we are currently in

```
% cd my_class/my_tasks
```

Once inside your newly created directory, we will begin to create new files. To create a file without editing the file we will use the **touch** command. This command will create a file if the file you specify does not exist. If the file does exist then this command will update the timestamp of the file as if you just updated the file. To initiate this process, let's begin by creating a file with the name "new_file". Afterwards, run the following commands to create this file:

```
% touch new_file
```

Now run the list command to view this new file

NOW YOU TRY THIS
Create the following 5 files
1. i_am_groot
2. program.bash
3. Yosemite.jpg
4. .hide_and_go_seek
5. .cant_find_me.txt

Run the Is command to view these files

Finally, take note! Not all of the newly created files were listed. This is because we created some hidden files as well. Any file or directory that starts with a period is considered a hidden file or directory. Look at the man pages for the Is command. Find the option that allows you to list all files, including hidden files. Go ahead and run the Is command with that option now to view all of the newly created files including the hidden files.

LAB TWO

INTRODUCTION TO THE LINUX ENVIRONMENT

In this chapter, you will be exposed to topics regarding the **terminal environmen**t. These topics include environment variables that you can utilize to help you as well as a profile file that helps to set up your environment to your liking. This chapter will also introduce you to file and directory permissions. You will also be introduced to a command line text editor.

By the end of this chapter, you should have a fair knowledge of the following objectives:

- Environment Variables
- File and Directory Permissions Including Changing Permissions
- File Types

Below are the commands introduced in this chapter:

- vi
- export
- source
- chmod
- umask

Throughout this lab, you will see three different color boxes. Each color indicates something different. A **BLACK** box indicates a command to run. A **GREEN** box indicates a question that you will need to answer. A **TURQUOISE** box tells you what to do on your own. An example of each follows:

A **BLACK** box will tell you what commands to run on your environment. Each black box is pre-seeded with a % sign. This sign is an example of a command prompt. DO NOT TYPE THE PRE-SEEDED % SIGN! Type only what follows the % sign.

A **GREEN** box will indicate a question. When answering questions you will need to run a command called 'read'. Type out exactly what is in a green box and then hit the «return› key. Once you see your question printed out onto the terminal, type out your answer. Hit the «returns key again to save your answer. If you make a mistake or if you want to type a different answer, just retype what is in the green box of the question.

```
read -p "Why is the sky blue? '' question[0]
```

A **TURQUOISE** box will give you a task to do on your own.

SAVING YOUR WORK WITH TYPESCRIPT

When submitting your task, you will be submitting a file called *Typescript*. This file contains a history of everything you have typed during your current SSH session. This is how you will prove that you have completed this lab.

Once logged onto the CIT 160 lab environment, run the following command to start the typescript.

```
% script
```

DO NOT CONTINUE UNLESS YOU GET THE FOLLOWING OUTPUT:

***Script* started, the file is typescript**

STAGE 1 I THE PATH ENVIRONMENT VARIABLE

Whenever you run a command on a server, how does it find it? Even though we see computers as being smart, someone or something had to tell them what to do and how. In our case, something needs to tell it exactly where to find the command you are trying to execute. This is where an environment] variable comes into play.

The PATH environment variable contains a listing of all the directories in the server that contain executable commands. If this variable did not exist then you would need to memorize each location command is located and type out the entire location. Let's do a test run so you can see how the PATH variable works.

Before we modify the PATH variable let's go ahead and back it up so we can restore it later without the need to log out and log back in.

```
% PATH_BACKUP= $ { PATH }
```

This command will save the current PATH variable into a new variable called "PATH_BACKUP". Before we completely blank out the PATH variable let's get the full path to two commands: ls and who. The ls command will list the contents of your current directory and who will display all logged-in users.

To view the full path to a command we will use a command called 'which'.

```
% which ls
% which who
```

Keep in mind the 2 directories that are printed out since we will be adding these directories back to the PATH variable.

Let's go ahead and blank out the PATH variable. After blanking it out we will try to run the 'ls' and 'who' commands and see what happens

```
% PATH= ""
% ls
```

Oh oh! The commands didn't exactly run did they. This is because the server does not know where to look for these commands. Let's fix this. We will add the path that was printed out for the ls command back into the PATH variable. To add it to the PATH variable run the following command. Replace/path/to_command with the actual path to the 'ls' command. Once you update the PATH variable try running the ls and who commands again. Do not include the actual command name at the end of the path.

```
% PATH= /path
% ls
% who
```

Did the ls command run this time? If it didn't you may need to redo the previous steps. Now did the who command run? It didn't right. This is because the 'who' command is in another directory. Let's update the PATH variable again but this time let's add in the path for the who command. Replace/path/to_command with the path to the who command. Do not include the actual command name at the end path.

```
% PATH=/path/to command
```

Ok, now let's recheck both commands again

```
% who
% ls
```

Looks like who ran correctly but the Is command did not run again. Why did it not run if we have updated our PATH variable to include it? Well, let's see. What we will do now is print out the contents of the PATH variable by using the echo command

```
% echo $ {PATH}
```

Hmm, well that is weird. There is only one directory in the PATH variable. Why is this? The reason for this is that we did not save the contents that were in the variable before. If you do not call the variable while saving it then the entire variable will get overridden. Let's add in the directory for the Is command again but this time we will save what is in the variable and then add in the new directory. Do not add in the actual command name at the end of the path.

```
% PATH= $ {PATH} :/path/to_command
```

Above we saved what was already saved and then added new content. With the PATH variable, each directory has to be separated by a colon (:). Now let's cross our fingers and run the 'ls' and 'who' commands one last time.

```
% ls
% who
```

Cool, both of them finally worked. If they did not then you may need to redo the above steps again.

Now you see how convenient the PATH variable is when it comes to running commands. Without it, you would need to remember the full path to every command available.

Let's go ahead and restore the original PATH variable value so that we don't run into problems later on. Remember the backup we made? We're gonna restore that now

```
% PATH= ${PATH_BACKUP}
```

STAGE 2 | PERMISSIONS

The CHMOD Command

Everything in Linux is controlled by permissions. These permissions are defined as who can do what and who owns what. Permissions are broken down into 3 groups: owner, group, and world. Each group is then further broken down into 3 permission bits: read, write, and execute. If you look at the long listing of files you will see in the first column the permission bits of each file and directory.

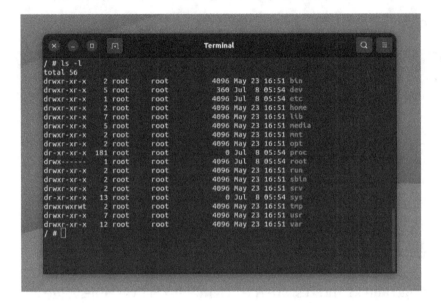

Let's break the long list down a bit to figure out the components of permissions

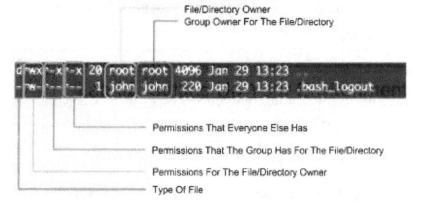

The first bit is the Type of File. Remember that everything in Linux is a file, including directories. The following are the different types of files available in Linux

File Bit	File Type
-	Regular File
d	Directory
b	Block File
c	Character Device File
p	Named pipe file or a pipe file
l	symbolic link list
s	socket file

The next 3 bits (orange box) are the permissions for the file owner. These permissions are broken down into **r**eading **w**rite e**x**ecute. This will be explained further in a bit.

The next 3 bits (cyan box) are the permissions for the file group owner.

The next 3 bits (lime green) are the permissions for everyone else.

The first name that you see is the username of the file owner. The second name that you see is the group. Anyone that is a part of the shown group gets the group permission bits. Now let's explain the **r**ead-**w**rite e**x**ecute bits

The read bit allows someone with the **r** bit to read the file

The write bit allows someone with the **w** bit to write to the file

The executable bit allows someone with the **x** bit to execute the file.

In the example above the .bash_history can be written and read by the file owner which in this case is john. The file can be read by the group john and can be read by everyone else.

SETTING PERMISSION BITS WITH CHMOD

There are 2 ways to set permission bits. The way shown here is using numbers. You set the permissions using the *chmod* command. What follows is a 3-digit number followed by the file/directory name. For example:

chmod 754 filename

The first number (7) controls what bits will be given to the owner. The second number **(5)** controls what bits will be given to the group owner. The third number (4) controls what bits are given to everyone else (world).

The question then is: how do you decide the right number to be used? We use the box model. The box model consists of 3 boxes, one for the read bit, one for the write bit, and one for the everyone else bit. An example of it is shown below

OWNER				GROUP				WORLD		
4	2	1		4	2	1		4	2	1
R	W	X		R	W	X		R	W	X

A deactivated permission bit has a 0 in the box so if no permissions are granted, you will have all 0's

OWNER				GROUP				WORLD		
4	2	1		4	2	1		4	2	1
R	W	X		R	W	X		R	W	X
0	0	0		0	0	0		0	0	0

Let's say we want to give the owner the read and write permission bits only. To do this, we activate those permission bits with a 1 for the owners box. The resulting box is

OWNER				GROUP				WORLD		
4	2	1		4	2	1		4	2	1
R	W	X		R	W	X		R	W	X
1	1	0		0	0	0		0	0	0

Now I'm sure you have noticed the numbers 4, 2, and 1 above the permission bits. We are going to use this to get the number to use with the chmod command. In this case, **R** and **W** are active with the binary number 1. So we add the above numbers (4+2) to get 6. So the first part of the chmod command is

chmod 6 filename

Now let's figure out the group owner permissions. We will give the group owner the read and execute permission. Our box will now look like this

Let's add the numbers. 4 + 1 Is 5 so the second number in the chmod command is 5. Now are command looks like this:

chmod 65 filename

Now let's get the last number. For everyone else, we will give them only read permissions so our box is

OWNER			GROUP			WORLD		
4	2	1	4	2	1	4	2	1
R	W	X	R	W	X	R	W	X
1	1	0	1	0	1	1	0	0

Only Read is active so our last number is 4.

Our final command is

chmod 654 filename

This is the command that we will run to give the file owner read and write permissions, the group owner read and execute permissions, and everyone else the read permissions. Sometimes you will see the chmod command with an extra 0 at the beginning as so:

chmod 0654 filename

The extra 0 is not necessary in our case but it does mean something. Either of these can be used to arrive at the same result. You must run the chmod command with either 3 digits or 4digits otherwise the command will not work.

Now let's get some hands-on experience with the chmod command.

11. First let's, make sure that we are in our home directory

```
% cd ; pwd
```

Make sure the printout is the PATH to your home directory, that is /home/user#/your_username

12. Create a new directory called 'sandbox' and change directories into it

```
% mkdir sandbox ; cd sandbox ; pwd
```

Make sure the printed result is /home/user#/your_username/sandbox

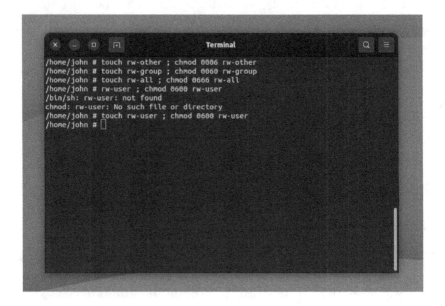

13. Now run the following commands to create a file and set new permissions for it.

```
        OWNER              GROUP              WORLD
      4   2   1          4   2   1          4   2   1
      R   W   X          R   W   X          R   W   X
    ┌───┬───┬───┐      ┌───┬───┬───┐      ┌───┬───┬───┐
    │ 1 │ 1 │ 0 │      │ 1 │ 0 │ 1 │      │ 0 │ 0 │ 0 │
    └───┴───┴───┘      └───┴───┴───┘      └───┴───┴───┘
```

```
% touch zero ; chmod 0000 zero
% touch rw-other ; chmod 0006 rw-other
% touch rw-group ; chmod 0060 rw-group
% touch rw-${USER} ; chmod 0600 rw-${USER}
% touch rw-all ; chmod 0666 rw-all
% touch rw-user ; chmod 0600 rw-user
```

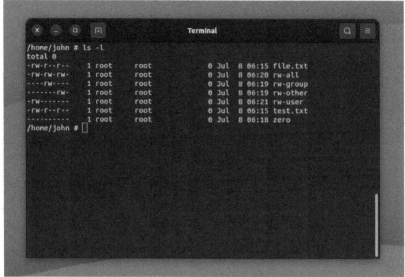

```
/home/john # ls -l
total 0
-rw-r--r--    1 root      root          0 Jul  8 06:15 file.txt
-rw-rw-rw-    1 root      root          0 Jul  8 06:20 rw-all
----rw----    1 root      root          0 Jul  8 06:19 rw-group
-------rw-    1 root      root          0 Jul  8 06:19 rw-other
-rw-------    1 root      root          0 Jul  8 06:21 rw-user
-rw-r--r--    1 root      root          0 Jul  8 06:15 test.txt
----------    1 root      root          0 Jul  8 06:18 zero
/home/john # 
```

14. Now run the list command with the options to display a long list, sort by time, and reverse the sort order

```
% ls -ltr
```

Notice the different permissions for each file.

15. Now let's clean up after ourselves. **Make sure you are inside your sandbox directory.** We will use a wildcard (*) to delete all files at once.

```
% rm -rf *
```

MAKING PERMISSION BITS WITH UMASK

There is a second command that deals with permissions. This command is the **umask**

command. This command controls what the permissions of a new file will be. **This**

command doesn't affect current files! It can only mask permissions for new files. This command is just like the chmod command in terms of how to set bits. We still use the box model to determine the 3-digit number. However, we use these numbers to mask permissions. What follows is the whole process of masking permissions with

Current file has the following permissions

owner			group			world		
4	2	1	4	2	1	4	2	1
R	W	X	R	W	X	R	W	X
1	1	1	1	1	1	1	0	1

We want to strip away the write permissions from the owner and group groups and get rid of all permissions from the world. To do this, we will mask those permissions.

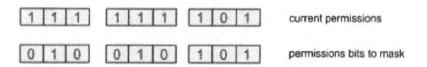

| 1 | 1 | 1 | 1 | 1 | 1 | 1 | 0 | 1 | current permissions |
| 0 | 1 | 0 | 0 | 1 | 0 | 1 | 0 | 1 | permissions bits to mask |

41

To calculate the umask value that we need, we use the box model using the permission bits to mask

| 4 | 2 | 1 | | 4 | 2 | 1 | | 4 | 2 | 1 |
R	W	X		R	W	X		R	W	X
0	1	0		0	1	0		1	0	1

2   2   4 + 1 = 5

Our command to mask the permission we wish to mask is

u*mask 225 filename*

Our resulting new file will have Read and Execute permissions for its owner, Read and Execute Permissions for its group owner, and no permissions for everyone else.

Linux will create a file or directory with full permissions, however, those permissions are stripped based on your current umask. To achieve your present umask, typing umask is all that is required of you to do. Try that now and then answer the questions that follow.

```
% umask
```

Let's go ahead and change our initial umask before creating some files so we can see its effects

Make sure you are still in the sandbox directory

```
% pwd
```

Run the following commands

```
% umask 0777 ; touch zero
% umask 0771 ; touch rw-other
% umask 0717 ; touch rw-group
% umask 0177 ; touch rw-${USER}
% umask 0111 ; touch rw-all
% umask 0177 ; touch rw-user
```

Let's list these files using long listing, sorted time, and reversed order

```
% ls -ltr
```

Notice the differences in permissions again.

JUST SOME MORE UMASK AND CHMOD PRACTICES

Let's let do some more examples to get the hang of permissions

```
% umask 0777; mkdir zero-dir
% umask 0377; mkdir read-dir
% umask 0577; mkdir write-dir
% umask 0677; mkdir exec-dir
% mkdir rw-dir ; chmod 0600 rw-dir
% mkdir rx-dir ; chmod 0500 rx-dir
% mkdir wx-dir ; chmod 0300 wx-dir
% mkdir rwx-dir ; chmod 0700 rwx-dir
```

Let's list our new directories

```
% ls -ltr
```

Now let's try to create some files in these directories. Some of these commands will give an error

```
% touch zero-dir/filename
% touch read-dir/filename
% touch write-dir/filename
% touch exec-dir/filename
% touch rw-dir/filename
% touch rx-dir/filename
% touch wx-dir/filename
% touch rwx-dir/filename
```

OTHER USES OF THE 'ls' COMMAND AND MORE PERMISSION EXAMPLES

The 'ls' command can be used to list the contents of other directories without actually changing directories to these directories. Let us now list the contents of all the directories contained within our current directories. Some will generate an error

```
% ls -l *
```

Now let's 'ls' a particular file inside of each directory

```
% ls -l */filename
```

Let's try listing the contents of a directory and listing a specific file

```
% ls wx-dir/filename
% ls wx-dir
```

You will notice in the above 2 commands, the former worked but not the latter.

Let's clean up after ourselves. **Make sure you are in the sandbox directory**

```
% pwd
```

If you are in the sandbox directory, run the following commands

```
% chmod 0777 *
% rm -rf *
```

Now let's return one folder to our home directory

```
% cd ..
```

Let's delete the sandbox directory

```
% rm -rf sandbox
```

CHALLENGE A

This challenge aims to teach you the following new commands:

- chmod
- umask
- export
- vi
- source

Using the **chmod** command, create the following Files or Directories within your home directory with the outlined permissions:

Type | Name	Owner	Group	World
File | Grid	R W X	R - X	R - -
File | Derezzed	R - X	- - -	- - -
File | Start_Wars	R W X	R - -	R - -
File | Light_Cycle	R - -	R - -	R W -
Directory | Disc_Winners	R W X	R - X	- - -
Directory | Avail_Cycles	R W X	R - X	R - X
Directory | Grid_Audio	R W X	R - X	- - -

Create A Directory Called "Lab2". Set The Permissions so that the owner has **R W X** permissions and all other groups have no permissions at all.

Move The Files and Directories Created Above [Grid, Derezzed, Start_Wars, Light_Cycle, Disc_Winners, Avail_Cycles, Grid_Audio] into the "Lab2" Directory.

Set Your **UMASK** value to 0043 and within your"Lab2" Directory, create the following files:

- Clu
- Tron
- Flynn

And Then Create The Following Directories:

- Encom
- Encom_OS_Sales

Verify the permissions of all Files and Directories within your"Lab2" Directory by issuing the "Is" command with the arguments to the long list and to show all files.

LAB THREE

THE TRUTH TABLE: DECIPHERING THE TEST COMMANDS

How does the system know something passed or failed? How can you test conditions? In this lab, you will learn how to see the status result of every command that you run. You will learn how to perform tests on integers and booleans. You will learn how truth tables work and their roles.

At the end of this chapter, you should have a fair knowledge of the following objectives:

- Boolean Values
- Base Operators
- Truth Tables
- Test Command
- '?' Environment Variable
- 'PROMPT_COMMAND' Environment Variable

Commands Introduced In This Lab

- test
- echo
- true
- false

Log onto your home lab environment or virtual lab environment by establishing an SSH connection with your favourite SSH client.

Once logged onto the lab environment, run the following command to start a typescript

```
% script
```

DO NOT CONTINUE UNLESS YOU GET THE FOLLOWING OUTPUT:

Script started, the file is typescript

STAGE 1: True and False: Boolean Values and Base Operators

For the following commands, you will be introduced to a new Environment Variable. This variable is the '?' variable. The '?' variable when echoed out will echo out the status of the last command. A status of 0 means the command ran successfully. It also means True. A status of 1 means the command did not run successfully. It also means False. Any other number means the command did not run successfully and a specific error occurred.

Let's see this variable in action.

```
% true ; echo $?
%false  ; echo $?
```

True returned a status of 0 and false returned a status of 1.

We can also negate (reverse) the boolean value by using an exclamation mark.

```
% ! true ; echo $?
% ! false  ; echo $?
```

In this case, true returned 1 and false returned 0.

You can also associate boolean values by wrapping them inside the parenthesis.

```
% (false)  ; echo $?
% (true) ; echo $?
% ! (false)  ; echo $?
```

So by now, I'm sure you're tired of typing 'echo $?' after every command. The bad news is that we still need to echo out the status for the entire lab. The good news is that we don't have to type it out after every command. In comes another   Environment   Variable   known   as   the

'PROMPT_COMMAND' variable. This variable gets executed after every command. By default the variable is empty. Let's replace it with the 'echo $?' command.

```
% PROMPT_COMMAND="echo $?"
```

Let's make sure this works

```
% true
```

Cool, that worked. Now Let's try with False

```
% false
```

Hmmm, we got a 0. Why didn't we get a 1? Let's echo out the PROMPT_COMMAND variable to find out

```
% echo $PROMPT_COMMAND
```

Based on consistent observation of it, a 0 will be voiced out. The reason for this is that we used weak quotes. Weak quotes will interpret variables then and there. This means that when we saved 'echo $?' being weak quotes used for the first time, the '$?' was interpreted as a 0 so the 0 was saved in its place. We don't want it to interpret then and there. We want it to interpret commands after they are issued, so we want to save 'echo $?' as is, without replacing

51

the '$?' with a 0. What we need to use are strong quotes. Strong quotes uses single quotes rather than double quotes. Without interpretation, Strong quotes will conceal the value. For us to save 'echo $?', the PROMPT_COMMAND variable with strong quotes will be used.

```
% PROMPT_COMMAND=' echo $? '
```

Now let's see how the PRoMPT_CoMMAND variable is stored and then retest True and False

```
% echo $PROMPT_COMMAND
% true
% false
```

Now we get the actual status. Remember what strong and weak quotes are because they will be really important when it comes to writing scripts. We can now continue with the rest of the lab.

STAGE 2: Truth Tables

Truth tables are tables that help determine what the result status will be. The last column in the Truth Tables (X) is for short-circuit evaluation. You'll see Short-Circuit evaluation in action further down the lab.

There are 2 truth tables. There is an AND (&&) truth table in which both conditions must be true for the result to be true. If one condition is false or both conditions are false then the result is false. AND Truth Tables can be defined by 2 ampersand symbols. The other truth table is an OR (||) truth table in which at least 1 condition needs to be true for the result to be true. OR Truth Tables can be defined by 2 pipe symbols. The short circuit evaluation column determines the final result when running a command. If you see an 'X' that means the final result is dependent on the result of the command. With the OR table, if the first condition is true and you run a command, the result will always be true. If the first result is False, then the result of the command will determine the final status result. With the AND table, if the first condition is False then the result will always be false, otherwise, the result will be determined by the result of the command. Both tables are shown below.

OR (||)	False	True	X
False	False	True	X
True	True	True	True

AND (&&)	False	True	X
False	False	False	False
True	False	True	X

Let's use the true and false boolean values to see the truth tables in action. Pay attention to the status code that is echoed out

```
% false || false
% false || true
% true || false
% true || true
% false && false
```

Now let's see the short-circuit results in action. We will be using a command that will always return an error. Do not create any directories. The command is supposed to fail

```
% cd foobar || cd foobar
% cd foobar || true
% true || cd foobar
% true || true
% cd foobar && cd foobar
% cd foobar && true
```

STAGE 3: Boolean Tests On Strings

Let's introduce you to the test command. On the premise of the flag presented to it, the test command performs a test. These tests can range anywhere from testing to see if something is a string, if a string is empty if a number is greater than or equal, and more. To view the complete outline of test flags, this is made possible by the man pages looking up the test command. For this lab, we will be focusing on string and integer tests.

A string is a collection of alphanumeric characters. Strings are usually saved in between double quotes. Let's run 3 tests on strings using different types of tests.

```
% test -z ""
% test -n "This is a string"
% test -z "This is a string"
```

These same tests can also be done on variables. Let's define two variables and then run the same tests on them.

```
% NULL= ""
% STRING= "This is a string"
% test -n ${NULL}
% test -n "${NULL}"
```

Why did I add weak quotes on the last command? You will see why in a bit. For now, let's run some more tests

```
% test -z "${NULL}"
% test -n "${STRING}"
% test -z "${STRING}"
% test "${STRING}" == "/bin/bash"
% test "${NULL}" != "/bin/bash"
```

There are also lexicographical tests that we can perform. For example, does the word "apple" appear before the word "oranges" in the dictionary. Because it does, the command "apple" < "oranges" should return true but it does not. We will see why later. For now, think about I/o redirection.

STAGE 4: Boolean Tests On Integers

We also can perform tests on numbers.

Let's define 2 variables to perform these tests. Set the 2 variables equal to whatever numbers you want. Do not add a space and do not add quotes. Adding quotes would change these integers into a string. Then run the following tests on these variables.

```
% n1=
% n2=
% test $n1 -eq $n2
% test $n1 -ne $n2
% test $n1 -gt $n2
% test $n1 -ge $n2
% test $n1 -lt $n2
% test $n1 -le $n2
```

LAB FOUR

PROMPT VARIABLE AND POSITIONAL VARIABLES IN BASH

Variables are used to store information that can be used later. You use variables by naming a variable and setting it equal to a value. For example, you can name a variable 'first_name' and give it the value 'john'. Now, every time you call the variable 'first_name' you will get the value 'john'. This is a nice way to remember information that may change over time. Instead of making the change in numerous locations, you just need to change the value stored in the variable. Variables can be used in many programming languages. Linux has a number of variables that are available upon logging on. These variables are known as environment variables. Each variable contains information pertaining to the current user, their environment, and more. This chapter will take you through some of these variables. You will then dip into the pool of BASH scripting.

By the time you finish this lab, you should have a fair knowledge of the following objectives:

- The Main Environment Variables:

-PSI

-1 - ∞ ARGUMENT POSITIONAL VARIABLES

- Basic BASH Scripting
- BASH Scripting Math Operations

Below are the commands introduced in this chapter

- vi (text editor)
- IF

Once logged onto your lab environment, run the following command to start a typescript

```
% script
```

DO NOT CONTINUE UNLESS YOU GET THE FOLLOWING OUTPUT:

Script started, the file is typescript

STAGE 1: The 'PROMPT' Environment Variable

As explained in the previous lab, the PROMPT is shown when the system is ready to take in a command. It consists of your username, server hostname, location, and a symbol. The PROMPT can, however, be changed by manipulating the 'PROMPT' variable. The prompt variable is 'PS1'.

3. Let's see what the current value for 'PS1' is. To read variables, we need to echo out its value. We do this by using the echo command followed by the variable name preceded by a t symbol. Run the following command to echo out the 'PS1' variable.

```
% echo $PSI
```

The output looks complicated. Since you won't need to memorize any of it. Let's try changing it. To change the prompt variable, we will need to replace the current data saved in 'PS1 with something else. To save data to a variable you type the variable name followed by an equal sign followed by the data to save. No spaces can exist before or after the equal sign. Just remember that when you read a variable you need to add the $ symbol before the name, but when saving data to a variable you do not add the $ symbol

4. Let's change the PROMPT to 'A Command I Am Ready For: '. Run the following command to replace the data in the 'PS1' variable

```
% PSI ="A Command I Am Ready For: "
```

Notice your new prompt? Go ahead and try giving it the 'pwd' command. As you can see the command will run and our new prompt is displayed once the system is ready to take in another command. This new prompt is not permanent. Environment variables do not hold their value once you log off so our change will be gone the next time we log back on. So how are Environment variables set when we log on? These variables are set by scripts that are executed upon every login. We'll keep our new prompt for the rest of this lab.

STAGE 2: 0-∞ Environment Variables

Another environment variable is the argument positional environment variable. Each argument given to a script and some commands, including the script or command name, is saved into an argument position variable. These variables are named integers. They can range from 0 to how many more arguments you pass onto a script. This works right, let's take a look into how this works

The Script name (calculator.bash) is saved into the argument positional variable 0. If we echo out 0 (echo $0) within the calculator.bash script will output 'calculator.bash'.

The '**4**' argument is saved into argument positional variable 1. If we echo out 1 (echo S1) within the plus.bash script will output '**4**'.

The '5' argument is saved into argument positional variable 2. If we echo out 2 (echo $2) within the plus.bash script it will output '5'.

Argument positional variables are useful when requiring input from a user. Instead of prompting the user to enter some input, you can just take in input by utilizing the argument positional variables.

Now let's see an example of how these variables can be used. In the next stage, we are going to write a simple bash script called 'calculator.bash' that takes in 2 numbers and displays the sum, difference, product, and quotient of these 2 numbers. We're going to write this script using a text editor called VI.

Recall the typescript you began at the commencement of this lab? We do not need to record what we do anymore so we can

```
% exit
```

You should get an output of

If you received this output you may continue to the next stage. If you did not get this output then it may be possible that you forgot to start the script when you began your lab. Contact your lab instructor or lab assistant to see what you should do from here.

STAGE 3: A Simple Calculator

Before continuing with this stage let's create a directory called 'Lab3'. This is where you will save the script for this lab. Make sure you are in your home directory before creating the Lab3 directory. Lastly, change into that directory. **Make sure that the capitalization of each letter matches what is shown here, otherwise you will run into problems when submitting.** Run the following commands to accomplish this. We'll knock them out all in one line by separating the commands with a ;

```
% cd - ; mkdir Lab3 ; cd ~/Lab3
```

Run the **pwd** command to verify that you are inside the 'Lab3' directory.

It's time to write your first script. We are going to use an editor called the vi editor. It is a text-based editor that runs on your terminal. Since we are going to name our script 'calculator.bash' we will run the vi command with the argument 'calculator.bash' that way it creates the file and opens the file for editing. If the file already exists then it will just open the file for editing. Run the following command to create the 'calculator.bash' file and open VI.

```
% vi calculator.bash
```

You should now be inside of the VI editor. To begin typing inside of VI you need to switch to "INSERT" mode. To switch into insert mode you need to type the letter L

```
I
```

The bottom of your terminal should now display the word "INSERT".

THE INTERPRETER

The first thing you have to do when you start a script is to declare what type of script you are writing. The very first line of a script needs to be the complete path to the interpreter you want to use to interpret your script. Interpreters include sh, php, python, bash, and others. For this class you will be using the BASH interpreter.

To start your script, type the following to declare BASH as the interpreter to use when executing your script

```
#! /bin/bash
```

Now hit the [ENTER] key to jump to the next line.

CHECKING THE POSITIONAL VARIABLES | A REGEX EXPRESSION | COMMENTING OUT CODE

The way we are going to run this script is by passing it 2 arguments, for example:

calculator.bash 4 5

just like what was shown in the previous stage.

So, the first thing we want to do in our script is to determine to see if the user inputted these 2 arguments and to check that the arguments are actual integers. We can knock both problems with one stone with the use of a regex expression. We are also going to use an IF statement to determine if they are integers or not.

The way we will use the IF statement is we are going to check the integers against the REGEX expression. IF the regex expression returns FALSE, THEN we will alert the user and exit the program with the status code of 1. Remember from the previous lab that 0 is true and 1 is false? In this case, 0 means a script ran successfully and anything greater than 0 means an error has occurred. In this case, we will use 1 as the error code. If the REGEX expression returns TRUE then we won't do anything and the script will move along to the code after the IF statement.

One last thing, since we are checking 2 variables we want our IF statement to check both at the same time. We will use an OR operation for this. So if variable 1 OR variable 2 are not valid integers, then return FALSE

We will also comment on our code so that we know what we are doing. To comment on a line of code you use a #. This tells the interpreter to skip this line. It is always good practice to use useful comments and almost any programming or scripting job will require you to comment on your code or else.

Go ahead and add the following comment and IF statement to your script. Make sure you type it exactly or it may fail. Note that the || are two pipes. Use the pipe key from your keyboard to enter them (Usually [Shift] + [\])

```
# Check the inputted arguments for a valid integer. Exit and alert if not.
if [[ ! $1 =~ ^[-+]?[0-9]+$ ]] || [[ ! $2 =~ ^[-+]?[0-9]+$ ]]; then
        echo "ERROR: One of the inputted values was not an integer. Good Bye"
        exit 1
fi
```

SAVING POSITIONAL VARIABLES INTo MEANINGFUL VARIABLES

Next, we want to save these variables into variable names that we will understand. Remember that the second positional variable (4) is saved to $1 and that the third positional variable (5) is saved to $2. We will save these variables into new variables called integer_one and integer_two. Type the following into your script to make this happen

```
Integer_one= $1
Integer_one= $2
```

MATH EXPRESSIONS

Now that we know the integers are valid we can go ahead and perform the math calculations. To perform a math calculation in BASH you need to use the following syntax

$((*MATH EXPRESSION*))

Examples:

To Add two Integers we use:

$((1 + 2))

To Add two integers saved into variables we use:

$((variable_one + variable_two))

And lastly to save the answer to a variable we use:

answer=$((variable_one – variable_two))

For our script, we are going to calculate the sum, difference, product, and quotient of the two inputted integers. We will save the answer into their variable with a meaningful name. For example, the sum of the two integers will be saved into a variable called *'sum'*

Copy the code below into your script. Remember to type it out exactly or your script will not work.

```
# Compute The Sum
sum=$(( integer_one + integer_two ))

# Compute The Difference
diff=$(( integer_one - integer_two ))

# Compute The Product
product=$(( integer_one * integer_two ))

# Compute The Quotient
quotient=$(( integer_one / integer_two ))
```

Math expressions can get more complicated. For example you can calculate expressions that contain parenthesis like so:

$(((integer_one + integer_two) - (integer_three + (4 + 5))))

RETURNING THE RESULTS

Finally, we want to return the results of our calculations to our user. We will use the echo command to do this. Since we are echoing out the value of a variable we will need to preseed the variable name with a $ symbol. Remember the following:

To Save Content To A Variable

Write the variable name, an equal sign, and then the content. For example **integer_one=3**
string_one= "Hello There"

To Read Content From A Variable

Write the variable name preceded by a $ symbol. The only exception to this rule is when the variable is inside of a math expression.

$integer_one
$string_one

We will return the results to the user as if they were a math expression. So we will echo out the first integer, the math operation, the second integer, an equal symbol, and the answer. Copy the following code to your script to do this.

We already did the calculations so all this will do is return the contents of the variables and won't calculate anything:

```
# Echo The Results
echo "${integer_one} + ${integer_two} = ${sum}"
echo "${integer_one} - ${integer_two} = ${diff}"
echo "${integer_one} * ${integer_two} = ${product}"
echo "${integer_one} / ${integer_two} = ${quotient}"
```

FINISHING YOUR SCRIPT

Our script is done but not quite done. To finish off the script we will add in an exit command and pass it the status of 0 meaning that this script ran successfully. Add the following to the end of the script

```
exit 0
```

EXITING VI

We are done. You can now get out of INSERT mode by hitting the [ESC] key. The INSERT word at the bottom of your terminal should go away. To save and exit your text document type the following

```
: wq
```

You will now return to the terminal

RUNNING YOUR SCRIPT

Now let's try to run our script. To run our script we are going to type out './' followed by the name of the script. The ./ tells the system to run the script located in your current working directory. **DO NOT USE THE SOURCE COMMAND TO RUN A SCRIPT. THIS IS NOT THE PROPER WAY TO EXECUTE A SCRIPT AND SOME SCRIPTS WILL NOT RUN CORRECTLY IF SOURCED.** The source command is used to integrate a script with your current environment. This is usually run when making changes to your local profile.

To run our scripts, type the following command

```
% ./calculator.bash  2Θ 4
```

WOAH! That wasn't what we expected. Looks like we don't have permission to execute our script. Don't worry this can be solved by running the chmod command as shown in the previous lab. By default, and for security reasons, a text file is not executable. So when we write a script we need to make the script executable for ourselves as well. To make our calculator script executable run the following command

```
% chmod +x  calculator.bash
```

The +× will add the executive permission bit to owner, group, and world. If you want to keep your script more private you can run chmod 0700 calculators.bash which will give you read, write, and execute permissions but will leave everyone else in the dark with no permissions.

Now let's try running our script again

```
% ./calculator.bash  20 4
```

Ahh, better, if all went well you should see the answers 24, 16, 80 and 5 in that order.

Now let's try out our regex expression to make sure it's checking for input and valid integers. Run the following commands to check this. They should all error out.

```
% ./calculator.bash
% ./calculator.bash   first 2
% ./calculator.bash   1 two
% ./calculator.bash   hello world
```

If the error message that we wrote was echoed out then you are good to go.

You will learn more about IF statements in the next lab.

CHALLENGE B

STAGE 1 | Lottery Winner

Create a script that will randomly generate 5 integers. Then, read in 5 user inputted integers. Check the integers to see if the user has won the lottery. The 5 randomly generated numbers should be between the numbers 1-5. You **do not** have to check the user input to verify that his/her number was between 1-5.

To generate a random number, use the $RANDOM variable. Example: $(((RANDOM % 5) + 1))). RANDOM will generate a random number starting from 0 and upwards. Because we also include %5, this number will range from 0-4. The + 1 is what will get our range from 1-5 by adding in an extra 1.

If the user did not win, echo out the winning numbers.

Name your script **lottery.bash** and save it inside of your home directory. Remember to give it executable permissions so that you can execute your script. **DO NOT SOURCE YOUR SCRIPT**

Test Case

Use the following test cases as an example of how your script should perform. Bolded text is user-inputted text.

```
% ./lottery.bash
Enter your first integer between 1-5: 3
Enter your second integer between 1-5: 4
Enter your third integer between 1-5: 1
Enter your fourth integer between 1-5: 5
Enter your fifth integer between 1-5: 5
Checking Your Results
I'm sorry but you are not a winner. The winning
numbers were 1,3,3,5,2. Please try again.
%./lottery.bash
Enter your first integer between 1-5: 2
Enter your second integer between 1-5: 2
Enter your third integer between 1-5: 5
Enter your fourth integer between 1-5: 3
Enter your fifth integer between 1-5: 1
Checking Your Results
YOU WON!
```

STAGE 2 | Uncle Sam

Uncle Sam is here knocking on your door waiting to collect your taxes. However, he doesn't necessarily know how much to collect from you. Let's create a script (to our advantage of course) that will help him decide how much to collect from us.

Your script should take in a user inputted integer of his/her gross pay per month. Once inputted, convert the per month gross pay to annual gross pay. Then use the following guidelines to determine how much taxes Uncle Sam will take from you.

If Annual Gross Pay is less than $10,000.00 **Then** Uncle Sam will take a flat rate of $545

If Annual Gross Pay is between $10,001.00 and $50,000.00 **Then** Uncle Sam will take 10% of your income.

 If Annual Gross Pay is between $50,001.00 and $12S,000.00 **Then** Uncle Sam will take 30% of your income plus an additional $1000.

If Annual Gross Pay is between $125,001.00 and $200,000.00 **Then** Uncle Sam will take 40% of your income plus an additional $3000.

If Annual Gross Pay is more than 200,001.00 **Then** Uncle Sam will take 10% of your income plus an additional $10,000.

Once all calculations are complete, echo out the user's monthly and annual gross income followed by taxes owed.

Name the script **taxman.bash** and save it in your home directory.

Test Case

Use the following test cases as an example of how your script should perform. Bolded text is user-inputted text.

```
% ./taxman.bash
How much was your monthly gross income?(Do Not Include $ , .): 24389

You made 24389 per month which amounts to 292668 per year.
You owe 39266 in taxes.

% ./taxman.bash
How much was your monthly gross income?(Do Not Include $ , .): 783

You made 783 per month which amounts to 9396 per year.
You owe 545 in taxes.

% ./taxman.bash
How much was your monthly gross income?(Do Not Include $ , .): 2100

You made 2100 per month which amounts to 25200 per year.
You owe 2520 in taxes.
```

LAB FIVE

NETWORKING COMMAND

One of the most widely used operating systems for various requirements and developments is Linux. Many programmers have used it in their development careers. Knowing the right command while working on Linux saves a lot of time and headache.

This chapter will cover 10 heavily used commands.

- ifconfig
- traceroute
- tracepath
- ping
- netstat
- hostname
- curl
- wget
- whois
- scp

However, I seek to streamline these commands to four.

1. **ifconfig:**
   This implies an **interface configurator**. This displays the configuration parameters for all active devices. The route and network interface are displayed using this command. It displays the configuration parameters of a single interface. For instance, **ifconfig ethΘ** displays the information on the interface etho. This command is also used for initializing an interface (up or down), configuring it with an IP address, and disabling or enabling it.

Syntax: **ifconfig**
ifcongfig interface down
Disables the interface. For example: **ifconfig ethΘ down.**
No traffic is sent or received on a disabled interface
ifconfig interface up
Enables an interface.
ifconfig **interface IPAdr/xx**
e.g. ifconfig **ethΘ 10.0.1.8/24**
Designates eth0 interface with the IP address 10.0.1.8/24
and 10.0.1.255 as a broadcast address
ifconfig ethΘ **mtu xxx**
Assigns MTU size xxx bytes to interface ethΘ
sudo echo 1 >'/proc/sys/net/ipv4/ip_forward'
        allows IPforwarding
sudo echo Θ > '/proc/sys/net/ipv4/ip_forward'
        disables IPforwarding
sysctl net.ipv4.ip_forward
        show current status of ipforwarding

2. **Traceroute:**
   When it comes to troubleshooting the network, traceroute
   is best suited. It detects the delay and also determines the
   pathway to the specified target. Traceroute performs the
   following functions
   - it makes available the names and identifies every device
     on the path
   - once the route is created, it follows it to the destination. It
     does this by sending messages back from all gateways in
     between the source and destination and increases the
     number each time by 1
   - it decides on where the network latency comes from and
     reports it

   traceroute IPaddr -mxxx -qyyy

Commands used to trace the route between an origin and a destination IP address IPaddr, where –m marks the max TTL value and –q indicates the number of queries e.g. m=2, and q=1

netstat-rnf : it shows the routing tables for IPv4

net.inet.ip.forwarding=1: allows forwarding of packets: (to convert a host into a router)

route add|delete [-net|-host]<destination><gateway> (ex. Route add 192.168.20.0/24 192.168.30.4) to add a route

route flush : it eliminates all the routes

route add-net 0.0.0.0 192.168.10.2 : to attach a default route

routed – Pripv2 –Pno_rdisc –d [-s|-q] to execute routed daemon with RIPv2 protocol, without ICMP auto-discovery, in, in supply or quiet mode

route add-net 224.0.0.0/4 127.0.0.1 : it defines the pathway used from RIPv2 **–n** : to query the RIP daemon on a specific host (manually update the routing table)

3. **Netstat**:
   In the process of computing, netstat is a command line tool that is used by most system administrators to evaluate network configuration and activity. It is also a valuable method of tracking or monitoring network activity and configuration.

   How to install Net-tools on Linux

Netstat is inclusive of a package called net-tools. It can be gotten from Ubuntu with the command below:

```
$ sudo apt install net-tools
```

```
aqsa@aqsa-VirtualBox:~$ sudo apt install net-tools
Reading package lists... Done
Building dependency tree
Reading state information... Done
net-tools is already the newest version (1.60+git20180626.aebd88e-1ubuntu1).
The following packages were automatically installed and are no longer required:
  libfprint-2-tod1 libllvm10 linux-headers-5.8.0-40-generic linux-hwe-5.8-headers-5.8.0-40
  linux-image-5.8.0-40-generic linux-modules-5.8.0-40-generic
  linux-modules-extra-5.8.0-40-generic
Use 'sudo apt autoremove' to remove them.
0 upgraded, 0 newly installed, 0 to remove and 5 not upgraded.
```

Verify tor version of Netstat

After installation, verify the version of the Netstat installed

```
$ netstat -v
```

```
aqsa@aqsa-VirtualBox:~$ netstat -v
Active Internet connections (w/o servers)
Proto Recv-Q Send-Q Local Address           Foreign Address         State
tcp       54      0 10.0.2.15:50536         111.68.98.122:8443      CLOSE_WAIT
tcp       54      0 10.0.2.15:50550         111.68.98.122:8443      CLOSE_WAIT
tcp        0      1 10.0.2.15:40326         35.224.170.84:http      SYN_SENT
tcp       54      0 10.0.2.15:50546         111.68.98.122:8443      CLOSE_WAIT
netstat: no support for `AF INET (sctp)' on this system.
netstat: no support for `AF INET (sctp)' on this system.
udp        0      0 localhost:39115         localhost:domain        ESTABLISHED
udp        0      0 10.0.2.15:47448         8.8.8.8:domain          ESTABLISHED
udp        0      0 10.0.2.15:39910         8.8.4.4:domain          ESTABLISHED
udp        0      0 10.0.2.15:44066         8.8.4.4:domain          ESTABLISHED
udp        0      0 10.0.2.15:50551         8.8.8.8:domain          ESTABLISHED
udp        0      0 10.0.2.15:38443         8.8.8.8:domain          ESTABLISHED
udp        0      0 10.0.2.15:34487         8.8.4.4:domain          ESTABLISHED
udp        0      0 10.0.2.15:bootpc        10.0.2.2:bootps         ESTABLISHED
udp        0      0 10.0.2.15:32862         8.8.8.8:domain          ESTABLISHED
udp        0      0 10.0.2.15:50796         8.8.4.4:domain          ESTABLISHED
udp        0      0 10.0.2.15:50808         8.8.8.8:domain          ESTABLISHED
udp        0      0 10.0.2.15:52894         8.8.8.8:domain          ESTABLISHED
udp        0      0 10.0.2.15:53023         8.8.8.8:domain          ESTABLISHED
udp        0      0 10.0.2.15:53219         8.8.8.8:domain          ESTABLISHED
udp        0      0 10.0.2.15:bootpc        10.0.2.2:bootps         ESTABLISHED
Active UNIX domain sockets (w/o servers)
```

The Netstat command in Linux displays a routine table

On the terminal, the Netsat command shows the routing table details. To see the routine table, use the −nr flag with Netstat; it displays the kernel routing table in the same way the route does. To achieve this, use the command shown below

```
$ netstat -nr
```

```
aqsa@aqsa-VirtualBox:~$ netstat -nr
Kernel IP routing table
Destination     Gateway         Genmask         Flags   MSS Window  irtt Iface
0.0.0.0         10.0.2.2        0.0.0.0         UG        0 0           0 enp0s3
10.0.2.0        0.0.0.0         255.255.255.0   U         0 0           0 enp0s3
169.254.0.0     0.0.0.0         255.255.0.0     U         0 0           0 enp0s3
```

Rather than using the symbolic names' address, the −nr option allows Netstat to print addresses divided by dots

Display interface statistics:

'-I' flag or option, once used with Netstat will display the statistics for configured network interfaces.

```
$ netstat -i
```

```
aqsa@aqsa-VirtualBox:~$ netstat -i
Kernel Interface table
Iface      MTU    RX-OK RX-ERR RX-DRP RX-OVR    TX-OK TX-ERR TX-DRP TX-OVR Flg
enp0s3     1500    2955      0      0 0          2639      0      0      0 BMRU
lo        65536    1172      0      0 0          1172      0      0      0 LRU
aqsa@aqsa-VirtualBox:~$
```

If the "-a" flag is combined with "-i", the command prints all of the kernel interfaces.

```
$ netstat -ai
```

```
aqsa@aqsa-VirtualBox:~$ netstat -ai
Kernel Interface table
Iface      MTU    RX-OK RX-ERR RX-DRP RX-OVR    TX-OK TX-ERR TX-DRP TX-OVR Flg
enp0s3     1500    2969      0      0 0          2652      0      0      0 BMRU
lo        65536    1172      0      0 0          1172      0      0      0 LRU
aqsa@aqsa-VirtualBox:~$
```

Display Network connection:

To view passive or active sockets, Netstat has a range of options. Active TCP, RAW, UDP and Unix sockets connections are specified by the –t, -u, -w, and –x options, respectively.

Type your terminal:

```
$ netstat -ta
```

```
aqsa@aqsa-VirtualBox:~$ netstat -ta
Active Internet connections (servers and established)
Proto Recv-Q Send-Q Local Address           Foreign Address         State
tcp        0      0 localhost:mysql         0.0.0.0:*               LISTEN
tcp        0      0 localhost:domain        0.0.0.0:*               LISTEN
tcp        0      0 localhost:ipp           0.0.0.0:*               LISTEN
tcp        0      0 0.0.0.0:db-lsp          0.0.0.0:*               LISTEN
tcp       54      0 aqsa-VirtualBox:50536   111.68.98.122.pern:8443 CLOSE_WAIT
tcp       54      0 aqsa-VirtualBox:50550   111.68.98.122.pern:8443 CLOSE_WAIT
tcp        0      0 aqsa-VirtualBox:54964   162.125.19.130:https    ESTABLISHED
tcp       54      0 aqsa-VirtualBox:50546   111.68.98.122.pern:8443 CLOSE_WAIT
tcp        0      0 aqsa-VirtualBox:56078   162.125.19.131:https    ESTABLISHED
tcp6       0      0 [::]:http               [::]:*                  LISTEN
tcp6       0      0 [::]:ftp                [::]:*                  LISTEN
tcp6       0      0 ip6-localhost:ipp       [::]:*                  LISTEN
tcp6       0      0 [::]:db-lsp             [::]:*                  LISTEN
aqsa@aqsa-VirtualBox:~$ 
```

Display Network Services

Run the following command to see a list of networks, their current states, and their associated ports:

```
$ netstat -pnltu
```

```
Active Internet connections (only servers)
Proto Recv-Q Send-Q Local Address           Foreign Address         State       PID
/Program name
tcp        0      0 127.0.0.1:3306          0.0.0.0:*               LISTEN      -

tcp        0      0 127.0.0.53:53           0.0.0.0:*               LISTEN      -

tcp        0      0 127.0.0.1:631           0.0.0.0:*               LISTEN      -

tcp        0      0 0.0.0.0:17500           0.0.0.0:*               LISTEN      303
5/dropbox
tcp6       0      0 :::80                   :::*                    LISTEN      -

tcp6       0      0 :::21                   :::*                    LISTEN      -

tcp6       0      0 ::1:631                 :::*                    LISTEN      -

tcp6       0      0 :::17500                :::*                    LISTEN      303
5/dropbox
udp        0      0 0.0.0.0:631             0.0.0.0:*                           -

udp        0      0 0.0.0.0:17500           0.0.0.0:*                           303
5/dropbox
udp        0      0 0.0.0.0:42123           0.0.0.0:*                           -
```

Display all Listening ports of TCP and UDP Connection:

By using this command below, you will be able to see all TCP and UDP ports

```
$ netstat -a | more
```

```
aqsa@aqsa-VirtualBox:~$ netstat -a | more
Active Internet connections (servers and established)
Proto Recv-Q Send-Q Local Address           Foreign Address         State
tcp        0      0 localhost:mysql         0.0.0.0:*               LISTEN
tcp        0      0 localhost:domain        0.0.0.0:*               LISTEN
tcp        0      0 localhost:ipp           0.0.0.0:*               LISTEN
tcp        0      0 0.0.0.0:db-lsp          0.0.0.0:*               LISTEN
tcp       54      0 aqsa-VirtualBox:50536   guestportal.hec.go:8443 CLOSE_WAIT
tcp       54      0 aqsa-VirtualBox:50550   guestportal.hec.go:8443 CLOSE_WAIT
tcp        0      1 aqsa-VirtualBox:34674   162.125.35.134:https    SYN_SENT
tcp        0      0 aqsa-VirtualBox:54964   162.125.19.130:https    ESTABLISHED
tcp       54      0 aqsa-VirtualBox:50546   guestportal.hec.go:8443 CLOSE_WAIT
tcp6       0      0 [::]:http               [::]:*                  LISTEN
tcp6       0      0 [::]:ftp                [::]:*                  LISTEN
tcp6       0      0 ip6-localhost:ipp       [::]:*                  LISTEN
tcp6       0      0 [::]:db-lsp             [::]:*                  LISTEN
udp        0      0 0.0.0.0:631             0.0.0.0:*
udp        0      0 0.0.0.0:17500           0.0.0.0:*
udp        0      0 0.0.0.0:42123           0.0.0.0:*
udp        0      0 0.0.0.0:mdns            0.0.0.0:*
udp        0      0 localhost:domain        0.0.0.0:*
udp        0      0 aqsa-VirtualBox:bootpc  _gateway:bootps         ESTABLISHED
udp6       0      0 [::]:41827              [::]:*
udp6       0      0 [::]:mdns               [::]:*
raw6       0      0 [::]:ipv6-icmp          [::]:*                  7
Active UNIX domain sockets (servers and established)
Proto RefCnt Flags       Type       State         I-Node   Path
unix  2      [ ACC ]     STREAM     LISTENING     38906    @/tmp/.ICE-unix/2632
unix  2      [ ACC ]     SEQPACKET  LISTENING     15204    /run/udev/control
unix  2      [ ACC ]     STREAM     LISTENING     15177    /run/systemd/private
unix  2      [ ACC ]     STREAM     LISTENING     39258    @/home/aqsa/.cache/ibus/dbus-mg1pj
```

Display TCP Port Connection:

Use the command below to access the list of TCP (Transmission Control Protocols) port connections:

```
$ netstat -at
```

```
aqsa@aqsa-VirtualBox:~$ netstat -at
Active Internet connections (servers and established)
Proto Recv-Q Send-Q Local Address           Foreign Address         State
tcp        0      0 localhost:mysql         0.0.0.0:*               LISTEN
tcp        0      0 localhost:domain        0.0.0.0:*               LISTEN
tcp        0      0 localhost:ipp           0.0.0.0:*               LISTEN
tcp        0      0 0.0.0.0:db-lsp          0.0.0.0:*               LISTEN
tcp       54      0 aqsa-VirtualBox:50536   guestportal.hec.go:8443 CLOSE_WAIT
tcp       54      0 aqsa-VirtualBox:50550   guestportal.hec.go:8443 CLOSE_WAIT
tcp        0      0 aqsa-VirtualBox:34674   162.125.35.134:https    ESTABLISHED
tcp        0      0 aqsa-VirtualBox:54964   162.125.19.130:https    ESTABLISHED
tcp       54      0 aqsa-VirtualBox:50546   guestportal.hec.go:8443 CLOSE_WAIT
tcp6       0      0 [::]:http               [::]:*                  LISTEN
tcp6       0      0 [::]:ftp                [::]:*                  LISTEN
tcp6       0      0 ip6-localhost:ipp       [::]:*                  LISTEN
tcp6       0      0 [::]:db-lsp             [::]:*                  LISTEN
```

Display UDP Port Connection:

Use this command to view the UDP (User Diagrams Protocols) port connection

```
$ netstat -au
```

```
aqsa@aqsa-VirtualBox:~$ netstat -au
Active Internet connections (servers and established)
Proto Recv-Q Send-Q Local Address           Foreign Address         State
udp        0      0 0.0.0.0:631             0.0.0.0:*
udp        0      0 0.0.0.0:17500           0.0.0.0:*
udp        0      0 0.0.0.0:42123           0.0.0.0:*
udp        0      0 0.0.0.0:mdns            0.0.0.0:*
udp        0      0 localhost:domain        0.0.0.0:*
udp        0      0 aqsa-VirtualBox:bootpc  _gateway:bootps         ESTABLISHED
udp6       0      0 [::]:41827              [::]:*
udp6       0      0 [::]:mdns               [::]:*
aqsa@aqsa-VirtualBox:~$
```

Display all Listening Connection

List all the active connections by using the "-I" flag with Netstat

```
$ netstat -l
```

```
aqsa@aqsa-VirtualBox:~$ netstat -l
Active Internet connections (only servers)
Proto Recv-Q Send-Q Local Address          Foreign Address         State
tcp        0      0 localhost:mysql        0.0.0.0:*               LISTEN
tcp        0      0 localhost:domain       0.0.0.0:*               LISTEN
tcp        0      0 localhost:ipp          0.0.0.0:*               LISTEN
tcp        0      0 0.0.0.0:db-lsp         0.0.0.0:*               LISTEN
tcp6       0      0 [::]:http              [::]:*                  LISTEN
tcp6       0      0 [::]:ftp               [::]:*                  LISTEN
tcp6       0      0 ip6-localhost:ipp      [::]:*                  LISTEN
tcp6       0      0 [::]:db-lsp            [::]:*                  LISTEN
udp        0      0 0.0.0.0:631            0.0.0.0:*
udp        0      0 0.0.0.0:17500          0.0.0.0:*
udp        0      0 0.0.0.0:42123          0.0.0.0:*
udp        0      0 0.0.0.0:mdns           0.0.0.0:*
udp        0      0 localhost:domain       0.0.0.0:*
udp6       0      0 [::]:41827             [::]:*
udp6       0      0 [::]:mdns              [::]:*
raw6       0      0 [::]:ipv6-icmp         [::]:*                  7
Active UNIX domain sockets (only servers)
Proto RefCnt Flags       Type       State         I-Node   Path
unix  2      [ ACC ]     STREAM     LISTENING     38906    @/tmp/.ICE-unix/2632
unix  2      [ ACC ]     SEQPACKET  LISTENING     15204    /run/udev/control
unix  2      [ ACC ]     STREAM     LISTENING     15177    /run/systemd/private
unix  2      [ ACC ]     STREAM     LISTENING     39258    @/home/aqsa/.cache/ibus
/dbus-mg1pjEMi
```

Showing Statistics by Protocol

Display protocol-specific statistics. The TCP, UDP, ICMP, and IP protocol statistics are displayed by default. A set of protocols can be using the –s option

```
$ netstat -s
```

```
aqsa@aqsa-VirtualBox:~$ netstat -s
Ip:
    Forwarding: 2
    3602 total packets received
    1 with invalid addresses
    0 forwarded
    0 incoming packets discarded
    3599 incoming packets delivered
    3917 requests sent out
    20 outgoing packets dropped
Icmp:
    178 ICMP messages received
    0 input ICMP message failed
    ICMP input histogram:
        destination unreachable: 178
    181 ICMP messages sent
    0 ICMP messages failed
    ICMP output histogram:
        destination unreachable: 181
IcmpMsg:
        InType3: 178
        OutType3: 181
Tcp:
    178 active connection openings
    0 passive connection openings
    4 failed connection attempts
    0 connection resets received
```

4. Curl

The curl command typifies "Client URL". It is a command line tool that enables data to be transferred over different network protocols (HTTP, FTP, IMAP, POP3, SCP, SFTP, SMTP, TELNET, TFTP, LDAP or FILE). To achieve this, it specifies a relevant URL and data to be sent or received by communicating with a web or application server. Curl is powered by Libcurl.

Syntax

```
Curl [options...] [URL..]
```

The most basic curl command is achieved by using this URL

curl https://www.geeksforgeeks.org

This will display the URL content on the terminal. This syntax is protocol-dependent and multiple URLs can be written as such:

curl http://site.{one,two,three}.com

By upgrading the packages, sometimes curl is already installed in Linux. It should be working by default, but if it is not installed, there is a simple installation method. This can be achieved by using a couple of commands.

After installation, the next thing is to update the already existing packages; thus enabling the repositories to install the curl in Ubuntu.

```
$ sudo apt update
```

```
aqsayasin@virtualbox:~$ sudo apt update
[sudo] password for aqsayasin:
Get:1 http://security.ubuntu.com/ubuntu focal-security InRelease [114 kB]
Get:2 http://ppa.launchpad.net/deadsnakes/ppa/ubuntu focal InRelease [18.1 kB]
Hit:3 http://pk.archive.ubuntu.com/ubuntu focal InRelease
Get:4 http://pk.archive.ubuntu.com/ubuntu focal-updates InRelease [114 kB]
Get:5 http://ppa.launchpad.net/ubuntu-mozilla-daily/ppa/ubuntu focal InRelease
[17.6 kB]
```

Curl Installation

Curl should be installed after enabling the repositories. To refresh the repositories might take some time though.

```
$ sudo apt install curl
```

```
aqsayasin@virtualbox:~$ sudo apt install curl
[sudo] password for aqsayasin:
Reading package lists... Done
Building dependency tree
Reading state information... Done
curl is already the newest version (7.68.0-1ubuntu2.5).
The following packages were automatically installed and are no longer required:
```

Ensure you ensure the right password to authenticate the installation. This process is quite easy to follow:

Check Version

Use the following statements in the Linux terminals to see the installed curl version. This will also verify the installation.

```
$ curl --version
```

```
aqsayasin@virtualbox:~$ curl --version
curl 7.68.0 (x86_64-pc-linux-gnu) libcurl/7.68.0 OpenSSL/1.1.1f zlib/1.2.11 bro
tli/1.0.7 libidn2/2.2.0 libpsl/0.21.0 (+libidn2/2.2.0) libssh/0.9.3/openssl/zli
b nghttp2/1.40.0 librtmp/2.3
```

The output above indicates that the installed curl version is 7.68

Example

The example below shows the content of the URL website on the Linux terminal by using this simple command.

$ curl URL

```
$ curl
https://ubuntu.com/download/desktop
```

```
aqsayasin@virtualbox:~$ curl https://ubuntu.com/download/desktop
<!doctype html>

<html prefix="og: http://ogp.me/ns#" class="" lang="en" dir="ltr">
<head>
  <meta charset="UTF-8">
  <meta name="viewport" content="width=device-width, initial-scale=1">

  <title>Download Ubuntu Desktop | Download | Ubuntu</title>

  <link rel="preconnect" href="https://res.cloudinary.com">
```

The output shows the HTML code of a specific website. This curl command can be used for more than one website. More than one URL can be written within the command.

curl http://site.{1st,2nd,3rd}.com

LAB SIX:

BASH SCRIPTING PART-LOOPS

Scripting is everything in the field of I.T. everything that you do will involve the usage of a script, either written by you or by someone else. A script is a collection of commands to execute in order. A script is useful when you want to achieve the same result across multiple systems. Examples are installing a package the same way on every system or simply automating the way you run maintenance.

Sometimes you want to govern which action you wish to take. In the previous lab, you were introduced to IF/ELSE statements. These statements are useful when you want to execute a certain action based on a parameter. IF this is true, then do action A; ELSE do action B.

What if you need to perform an action X amount of times? X can be anything from 0 times to 1,000 times. Enter Loops. In this lab, you will be introduced to 2 different kinds of loops that you can utilize whenever you aren't sure of how many times a certain block of code should execute.

At the end of this chapter, you should have a fair understanding of the following topics:

- While Loops

- For Loops

Here are the commands Introduced In this Lab:

- do

- done

- while

WHAT'S A LOOP

A loop is a segment of code that runs continuously for as long as the condition for the loop remains true. The loop is broken once the condition returns false. In BASH there are 2 main types of loops: *for, while.*

WHILE LOOP

A while loop contains the following:

```
while [[ test_cond_is_true ]]; do

    # Code To Loop

done
```

For this stage, we are going to write a script that continues to prompt the user to guess the correct number until he/she guesses the correct number.

Create a new file called Guess Number using the vi editor.

You must always declare your interpreter, that's your starting off script point.

```
#!/bin/bash
```

Next, we will want to generate a random number to check against. We will prompt the user to guess a number between 0 and 15 so we will set the RANDOM variable to get a random number between 0 and 15. We will save the winning number to a variable called 'winning number'.

```
Winning_number=$[( RANDOM % 15 )]
```

Now to start the loop we will need to set another variable. We will call this variable 'user guess'. In order for the loop to start, we will set this number to a number outside of the range of winning numbers. Let's do that now

```
Use_guess=16
```

Alright, now it's time to start the loop. This loop needs to run so long as the user does not guess the correct number. So what we want to do is while f (user guess) is not equal to $(winning number) we want to prompt the user to guess a number.

Our while loop will start as follows

```
while [( ${user_guess} -ne ${winning_number} )]; do
```

Next, we will prompt the user to guess a number between 0 and 15. We will use the read command to do this and we will save their answer in the 'user guess' variable.

```
reap -p "Guess a number between 0 and 15:" user_guess
```

Now let's check the 2 numbers. **If** they are not equal to each other, **then** alert the user that the guess was incorrect. This smells like an IF statement. Let's add it in now.

```
if || $(user guess) -ne $(winning number} ]j; then
    echo "Your guess, $(user guess}, was incorrect. Please try again."
fi
```

We will then end the loop

```
done
```

As long as the guess is wrong, this loop will continue. Once the user guesses the correct number this loop will stop. Let's write the code that comes after the loop. We will want to congratulate the user for guessing the correct number.

```
echo "Congrats! Your guess ,${user_guess}, was correct :)"
```

And like always, end a script with the exit status.

```
exit 0
```

Below should be the new look of your script

```
#!/bin/bash

# Our Variables
winning_number=$(( RANDOM % 15 ))
user_guess=16 # A number out of range of the winning number so the loop will start

# Loop While User Guess Is Wrong
while [[ ${user_guess} -ne ${winning_number} ]]; then
    read -p "Guess a number between 0 and 15: " user_guess
    # Check number. If wrong, alert the user to try again
    if [[ ${user_guess} -ne ${winning_number} ]]; then
        echo "Your guess, ${user_guess}, was incorrect. Please try again."
    fi
done
echo "Congrats! Your guess ,${user_guess}, was correct! :)"
exit 0
```

LAB CHALLENGE A

SCRIPT 1 Create a script that will take in x amount of numbers from a user (minimum 5 numbers) via the use of positional variables. Then do the following:

- Count how many numbers were inputted

- Add up all the numbers

- Multiply all the numbers

- Find the average of all the numbers

Finally, echo out this information back to the user, including the numbers inputted. Name your scrip *math_helper.bash*

Test Case Bolded Text Is User Inputted Text

```
% ./math_helper.bash 3 8 1

Error: I'm sorry but I need 5 integers to
work. You only entered 3. Try Again.

% ./math helper.bash 4 9 8 2 5 You entered 5
numbers.

The Sum of 4 9 8 2 5 is 28.

The Product of 4 9 8 2 5 is 2880. The Average
Is 5.
```

SCRIPT 2 Create a script that will take in a number from a user. This script should first check if a number was provided via a positional variable. If no number was provided, then prompt the user for a number. onIy 1 number is required. Once you have received the user's input, create a half triangle using asterisks (*) in the form of a countdown as shown in the test case below. Name this script **triangle.bash.**

```
% ./triangle.bash 4

* * * *

* * *

* *

*
```

Test Case

Bolded Text Is User Inputted Text

HINTS

Command arguments are saved and read by scripts as positional variables. Positional variables start at the number 0 and continue on for as many arguments that a user provides. For example a command like:

```
%./meth_compute.bash 4 3 9
```

will have 4 positional variables assigned as follows:

$0 => math_compute.bash

$1 => 4

$2 => 3

$3 => 9

```
%  ./triangle .bash

Please enter a number: 7

* * * * * *

* * * * * *

* * * * *
```

Positional variables also include the following shortcuts:

$@ => Echos out all inputted integers after variable 0.

$# => Returns the total number of positional variables after variable 0.

So for the above command:

$@ **would return** 4 3 9

$# **would return** 3

You can use the shortcuts above to help you out when creating your for loops and when checking to see if the user has inputted anything via positional variables with the use of an IF statement.

LAB CHALLENGE B

SCRIPT 1 Create a script that will take in x amount of numbers from a user (minimum 5 numbers) via the use of position

al variables. Then do the following:

- Add All Even Number Integers Together

- Multiply All Odd Number Integers Together

- Subtract The Sum From The Product

- Determine The Average For All Numbers

Finally, echo out this information back to the user, including the numbers inputted. Name your script

math_rocks.bash

Test Case **Bolded Text Is User Inputted Text**

```
% ./math rocks.bash 7 9 10

Error: I'm sorry but I need 5 integers to
work. You only entered 3. Try Again.


% ./math_rocks.bash 42 33 1 13 4 7 9 3 8 You
entered 9 numbers.

The Sum of 42 4 8  is 54.

The Product of 33 1 13 7 9 3 is 81081.

The Difference Of 81081 - 54 is 81027 The Average
Is 13.
```

SCRIPT 2 Create a script that will take in a number from a user. This script should first check if a number was provided via a positional variable. If no number was provided, then prompt the user for a number. Only 1 number is required. Once you have received the user's input, create a half triangle using integers in the form of a countdown timer as shown in the test case below. Name this script **triangIe_up.bash.**

Test Case **Bolded Text Is User Inputted Text**

```
%  ./triangle_up.bash 7
7 6 5 4 3 2 1
6 5 4 3 2 1
5 4 3 2 1
4 3 2 1
3 2 1
2 1
1

%
./t
ria
ngl
e
up.
```

HINTS

Command arguments are saved and read by scripts as positional variables. Positional variables start at the number 0 and continue for as many arguments that a user provides. For example a command like:

```
%. /match_rocks .bash  4 3 9
```

will have 4 positional variables assigned as follows:

$0 => math_rocks.bash

$1 => 4

$2 => 3

$3 => 9

Positional variables also include the following shortcuts:

$@ => Echos out all inputted integers after variable 0.

$# => Returns the total number of positional variables after variable 0.

So for the above command:

$@ **would return** 4 3 9

$# **would return** 3

You can use the above shortcuts to help you out when creating you're for loops and when checking to see if the user has inputted anything via positional variables with the use of an IF statement.

LAB SEVEN:

BASH SCRIPTING - IF STATEMENTS

LAB CHALLENGE A

STAGE 1 | Lottery Winner

Create a script that will randomly generate 5 integers. Then, read in 5 user inputted integers. Check the integers to see if the user has won the lottery. The 5 randomly generated numbers should be between the numbers 1-5. You **do not** have to check the user input to verify that his/her number was between 1-5.

To generate a random number, use the $RANDOM variable. Example: $(((RANDOM % 5) + 1))). RANDOM will generate a random number starting from 0 and upwards. Because we also include %5, this number will range from 0-4. The + 1 is what will get our range from 1-5 by adding in an extra 1.

If the user did not win, echo out the winning numbers.

Name your script **lottery.bash** and save it inside of your home directory. Remember to give it executable permissions so that you can execute your script. **DO NOT SOURCE YOUR SCRIPT**

Test Case

Use the following test cases as an example of how your script should perform. Bolded text is user-inputted text.

```
% ./lottery.bash
Enter your first integer between 1-5:
3 Enter your second integer between 1-
5: 4 Enter your third integer between
1-5: 1  Enter your fourth integer
between 1-5: 5  Enter your fifth
integer between 1-5: 5
Checking Your Results
I'm sorry but you are not a winner. The winning
numbers were 1,3,3,5,2. Please try again.
%./lottery.bash
Enter your first integer between 1-5: 2 Enter
your second integer between 1-5: 2 Enter your
third integer between 1-5: 5 Enter your fourth
integer between 1-5: 3  Enter your fifth
integer between 1-5: 1
Checking Your Results
YOU WON!
```

STAGE 2 | Uncle Sam

Uncle Sam is here knocking on your door waiting to collect your taxes. However, he doesn't necessarily know how much to collect from you. Let's create a script (to our advantage of course) that will help him decide how much to collect from us.

Your script should take in a user inputted integer of his/her gross pay per month. Once inputted, convert the per month gross pay to annual gross pay. Then use the following guidelines to determine how much taxes Uncle Sam will take from you.

If Annual Gross Pay is less than $10,000.00 **Then** Uncle Sam will take a flat rate of $545

If Annual Gross Pay is between $10,001.00 and $50,000.00 **Then** Uncle Sam will take 10% of your income.

If Annual Gross Pay is between $50,001.00 and $12S,000.00 **Then** Uncle Sam will take 30% of your income plus an additional $1000.

If Annual Gross Pay is between $125,001.00 and $200,000.00 **Then** Uncle Sam will take 40% of your income plus an additional $3000.

If Annual Gross Pay is more than 200,001.00 **Then** Uncle Sam will take 10% of your income plus an additional $10,000.

Once all calculations are complete, echo out the users' monthly and annual gross income followed by taxes owed.

Name the script **taxman.bash** and save it in your home directory.

Test Case

Use the following test cases as an example of how your script should perform. Bolded text is user-inputted text.

```
% ./taxman.bash
How much was your monthly gross income?(Do Not Include $ , .): 24389

You made 24389 per month which amounts to 292668 per year.
You owe 39266 in taxes.

% ./taxman.bash
How much was your monthly gross income?(Do Not Include $ , .): 783

You made 783 per month which amounts to 9396 per year.
You owe 545 in taxes.

% ./taxman.bash
How much was your monthly gross income?(Do Not Include $ , .): 2100

You made 2100 per month which amounts to 25200 per year.
You owe 2520 in taxes.
```

LAB EIGHT

THE WORLD RUNS ON DNS

What is DNS

DNS is a service that is used to translate human-readable web addresses into an IP Address. It allows us, humans, to use URLs like www.google.com to get to the website we want instead of having to memorize an IP Address like 74.125.239.9 or 2607:f8b0:4007:801 :1006. So it's pretty much the yellow pages of the Internet.

The Domain Name Service is an application that resides on a server. This server is known as the DNS server. A DNS Server usually resides in every network on the Internet. Your Internet Service Provider may have a DNS server that your computer connects to a school that has a DNS server, and your wireless router at home may even have a built-in DNS server. Networks tike Facebook need DNS servers to help get you to the right server on their network.

UNDERSTANDING DNS ZONE FILE

What is a DNS Zone File?

A zone file is a file that contains records about a network. It allows someone on the Internet to get to the server they want to reach. Think of it as an entry in the yellow pages. A zone file can contain any of the following records

- **NS** - Name Server o Maps to the DNS server of a network. An A or AAAA record is required to map to the IP Address of the DNS Server. The NS record only contains the DNS server hostname

- **MX** - Mail eXchange o Maps to the mail exchange server of a network. An A or AAAA record is required to map to the EP Address of the Mail Exchange server. The MX record only contains the MX server hostname and a priority number.

- **TXT** - Text Record o Contains a comment OR contains additional information that is used to associate a zone file with specific services. For example, Google Apps for Businesses uses a TXT record that you place into your zone file to authenticate that your network is really your network.

- **PTR** - Pointer Record oThe reverse of an A Record. Maps an IP Address to a hostname. There should be the same amount of PTR records as there are A records.

- **CNAME** - Common Name oAn alias record that points to a server on the network. For example, if your web server is named 'Cortana', you can add a CNAME record of 'www' to point to that web server.
- **A** - A Record o A record that maps a hostname to an IPv4 Address that points to that server.
- **AAAA** - AAAA Record o A record that maps a hostname to an IPv6 Address that points to that server.

A zone file also contains an SOA or Start of Authority. The SOA includes the following:

Your Primary DNS Server

The Webmaster's Email Address In The Form Of A URL

The Serial Number

o This acts as the Zone Files Version Number. It should be incremented every time you update your zone file.

Refresh Rate

o The time for when a stave DNS server should refresh its information about the zone file

Retry Rate

o The time that a server should retry refreshing the zone file if a refresh fails.

• Expire Time

o The time that the zone file will expire forever on that server

Minimum

o The minimum amount of time a zone file should be cached. The time for the refresh, retry, expire, and minimum times should be listed as seconds. The last page of this workspace contains a sample zone file.

Your Network Outline

When configuring your zone files, use the following network diagram. ONLY PRIVATE IP ADDRESSES should be assigned to any server in the Intranet (Red Zone) (10.160.x.x where x is replaced with any number from 1-254.). In the DMZ (Green Zone), any server should have BOTH PUBLIC AND PRIVATE IP ADDRESSES. To assign public IP addresses, use the Public IP Address range that was assigned to you when you registered your domain. A server can have any hostname as long as it is appropriate. BE INNOVATIVE!

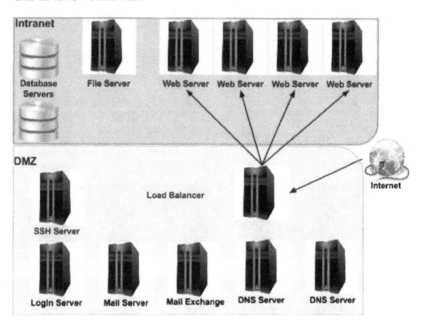

```
$TTL 3600
;$ORIGIN cit160agent.gov.
@  IN  SOA  map.citagent.gov. joshua.citagent.gov. (
   2014100800  ; serial
   28800      ; refresh (8 hours) when the slave DNS server refreshes info
   14400      ; retry (4 hours) upon failed slave connection
   604800     ; expire (1 week) cached information in the slave
   86400      ; minimum (1 day) time to cache (not consult)data in files
        )

;; NS Records
   NS map
   NS gps

;; MX Records
   IN MX 10 postoffice
   IN MX 20 postalworker

;; Add A & CNAME Records for Public Servers (Accessible From Internet)
map        A    240.160.4.10
gps        A    240.160.4.11
postoffice A    240.160.4.20
postalworker A    240.160.4.21
cortana    A    240.160.4.30
www        CNAME cortana
;; Add The Rest of your Public A Records & CNAMES (if any) Here

;; PTR Records For All Public IP Address A Records Go Here
240.160.4.10  PTR   map

;; Add A & CNAME Records for Private Servers (Accessible From Intranet)
map        A    10.160.3.1
gps        A    10.160.3.2
postoffice A    10.160.2.1
postalworker A    10.160.2.2
cortana    A    10.160.1.1
www        CNAME cortana
chief      A    10.160.4.1
;; Add The Rest OF Your Private A Records & CNAMES (if any) Here

;; PTR Records For All Private IP Address A Records Go Here

;; Your 253 Generic A Records Go Here
```

LAB NINE

INTRODUCTION TO EMAIL- THE CURL COMMAND

Welcome to the world of email. Ever since its creation, email has been becoming the primary source of everyday mail from bills to coupons to spam. Until the advent and wide acceptance of social media sites and text messaging, it was the quickest medium of communicating with someone. This lab will introduce you to sending and reading email messages using the Linux terminal.

Lab Objectives

At the end of this Lab, you should have attained a certain degree of the following objectives:

1. Learn how to read email using the command line
2. Learn how to send email using the command line
3. Use curl to send and receive email

Commands Introduced In This Lab

- mail
- curl

Sending and reading e-mails using a Linux terminal

- To start the terminal, press CTRL+ALT+T

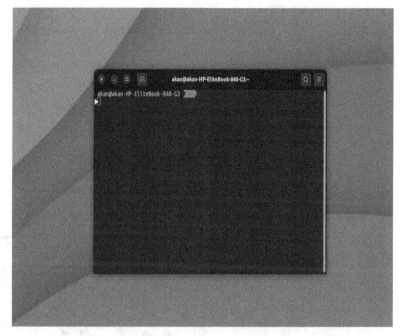

- We'll start by downloading curl that we will be using to send the mails
- Run "sudo apt update" to update your local repository
- Next, run "sudo apt install curl" to install curl as that's going to be the package in use.

For this lesson, we will be using mailinator to send and receive emails. So head on to mailinator and create your test disposable email

From the above image, we created two test mail accounts, one to send the email, and the other to receive, click on the go button to go to your inbox.

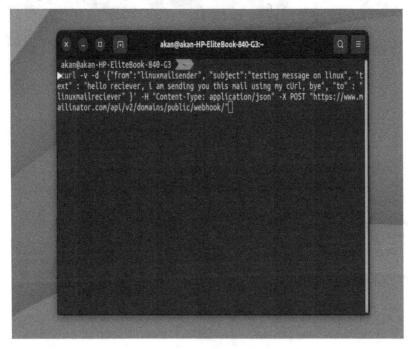

As we can see our receiver got his email

LAB TEN

BROWSING THE WEB WITH CURL

For starter let us try to open the famous google on our curl

Browsers automatically follow redirects, so this requested page will only be available for a microscopic fraction of time before the redirected version of the page is loaded. CURL, by default, does **NOT** follow redirects, so you get that intermediate page instead.

But if we try to open a page which does not require a redirection, we can get back all the necessary program files embedded in the HTML file. These include some inline styling, embedded scripts, and the HTML skeletal markup itself, for example

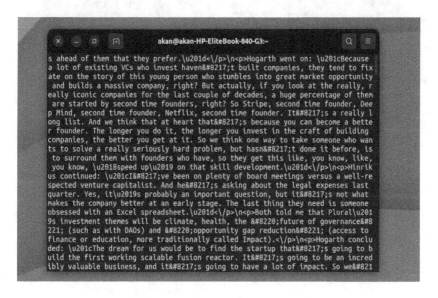

stNonce":null},"isLoginLocked":"","initialStore":{"events":{"eventTypeIDs":[],"eventPostIds":[],"featuredEventIDs":{"event_home":[]},"featuredPostIDs":{},"pastEventIDs":{"default":[]},"pastFilters":{},"pastLoading":false,"upcomingEventIDs":{"default":[2341982,2341556,2328170,2244054,2205927]},"upcomingFilters":{},"upcomingLoading":false},"terms":[],"videoIdsByPlaylist":{"playlists":[]}},"headlessSubpageSlugs":["tickets","exhibitor-directory"],"extraCrunchMarketingPageURL":"\/subscribe","brandStudioMarketingPageURL":"\/brand-studio","newsletterURL":"https:\/\/link.techcrunch.com\/join\/134\/signup-all-newsletters"};

On the above images, we can see we were able to get back the recent blog posts available on the TechCrunch website, and also some embedded javascript.

Similarly, we could also retrieve the header file of a page to know the expected request type we are making (GET, POST, etc) and other parameters such as the content type.

```
akan@akan-HP-EliteBook-840-G3:~
akan@akan-HP-EliteBook-840-G3
curl --head https://techcrunch.com
HTTP/2 200
server: ATS
date: Tue, 28 Jun 2022 03:24:28 GMT
content-type: text/html; charset=UTF-8
content-length: 1085449
x-hacker: If you're reading this, you should visit wpvip.com/careers and apply t
o join the fun, mention this header.
x-powered-by: WordPress VIP <https://wpvip.com>
host-header: a9130478a60e5f9135f765b23f26593b
content-security-policy: default-src https: 'unsafe-inline' 'unsafe-eval' blob:;
img-src * data: https:; object-src 'none'; connect-src https: wss:; script-src
'unsafe-inline' https: 'unsafe-eval'; worker-src 'self' blob:; upgrade-insecure-
requests; block-all-mixed-content; sandbox allow-forms allow-same-origin allow-s
cripts allow-popups allow-popups-to-escape-sandbox allow-presentation; media-src
'self' blob: data: https:; font-src 'self' data: https://use.typekit.net https:
//cdn.vidible.tv https://cdnjs.cloudflare.com https://fonts.gstatic.com https://
s0.wp.com ;
referrer-policy: no-referrer-when-downgrade
link: <https://techcrunch.com/wp-json/>; rel="https://api.w.org/"
x-rq: lhr3 0 2 9980
cache-control: max-age=300, must-revalidate
age: 452
```

```
age: 452
x-cache: hit
vary: Accept-Encoding
accept-ranges: bytes
strict-transport-security: max-age=31536000
expect-ct: max-age=31536000, report-uri="http://csp.yahoo.com/beacon/csp?src=yah
oocom-expect-ct-report-only"
x-content-type-options: nosniff
x-xss-protection: 1; mode=block
x-frame-options: SAMEORIGIN

akan@akan-HP-EliteBook-840-G3
```

So from the above images, we can also see the technologies (WordPress CMS) which were used in building our test website. We can also see that some necessary measures were taken to prevent cross-scripting and XSS attacks by hackers. We can also see that the web server is running on an ATS server.

LAB ELEVEN:

UNDERSTANDING LOGS, CRON JOBS, CRON TABS , AND SSH KEYS

It's time to calm things down and show you some of the great tools that you will need for your I.T careers. The first one is logged. Logs can aid in figuring out what is wrong with a server or if anyone has gained unauthorized access to it. The second is Cron jobs. Cron jobs can aid in the automation of everyday tasks. Lastly, there are SSH keys. SSH keys can heighten the security of a server when used responsibly.

LAB GOALS

In this lab you will:

- Learn about and analyze log files
- Learn about and create a cron job via crontab
- Learn about how to setup SSH keys and how to use them responsibly
- Learn about the curl command

STAGE 1 Creating A Script For The Crontab I The 'Curl' Command

First, create a directory called 'logs' within your home directory. This is the location where we will save our outputted logs.

To get started with log files and log rotations, we'll create a script in our home directory that will log its output. This script will be named 'IsTheServerUp.bash.' The script will, as the name suggests, check to see if a server is up and running. It will then log (echo) the script's output to a file. We'll use the curl command to see if a server is up and running.

The curl command is a command that connects to a URL and transfers data from it. The data to transfer depends on how the command is run but by default, it will retrieve the HTML document of a web page.

To write your bash script, the following set of rules should be used:

- Use the 'curl' command to request a web page from the server
- e.g, curl "http://www.un.org/" (You can use whatever webpage you want) . provide the '-output /dev/null option + argument to suppress output

- Check the return status ($?) to determine if there is a problem
- Perhaps the returned status reads 'o', log success message to the file. If the returned status is not 'o, log an error message to the file. Ensure the status code and date/time stamp are included. An example can take this outlook: (the date/time stamp formatting style can be checked on the man page)

-
```
Apr-11-2015-04.12:00 PM (0) Web Server [ www.xbox.com ] Is Online
Apr-11-2015-08.39:00 PM (7) Web Server [ www.xbox.com ] Is Offline
```

- In your newly created 'logs' directory, Log your outputted messages to a file called 'Server_lnfo.log'.

STAGE 2 | Organizing A Cronjob With Crontab

For this lab section, we will develop another script and add a cron job.

Write a script called 'log_copy'. This script should be run every hour via a cron job. It will take as input the log file from the previous bash script. One method is to "grep" the log file for information that matches a timestamp within the last hour. To construct this BASH script, follow these outlined hints.

1 . Determine what the last hour is and save it as a variable as shown below (check date man page)

```
LAST_HOUR="$(( $(date +%l) - 1 ))"
```

if LAST-HOUR is less than 10 then pad a 0 in front

i.e.: 6 should become 06

2 . Create the search string and save it as a variable as shown below

```
SEARCH_STRING=$(date +"%b-%d-%Y-${LAST_HOUR}:")
```

The above string will search through your 'Server-Info.log' file for timestamps matching the last hour.

3 . Search the log file with the following command inside of your 'log-copy' script.

```
grep "${SEARCH_STRING}"
```

4 . Output the results to a new log file. Name this new log file 'Server_Hourly.log'. Make sure that this new log file is located inside your 'togs' directory and that the script 'log_copy' is located inside your home directory.

5 . Upon the creation of both scripts, verify them by first running the 'IsTheServerUp.bash' script. Make sure a log file called 'Server_Info.log' was saved inside of your 'logs' directory after running this script. When you see that

a log file has been created and is dominated by the script's output, you can run your 'log copy' script. Following the execution of your second script, ensure that a second log file called 'Server Hourly.log' was created in your 'logs' directory and that it is dominated by the outputs of the second script.

6.   You will need to create 2 cron jobs once both script works have been verified so that automagically, these scripts are running. Develop a fresh cron job by running the following command:

```
% crontab -e
```

NOTE: Select the first editor should you be prompted to select an editor, (Option 1 - /usr/bin/vim/basic)

Add the following rules to your crontab:

- At the interval of 10 minutes, Run your 'IsTheServerUp.bash' script.
- Run your 'log_copy' script every hour.
- Make sure you add the entire path to your script so /home/users#/your-username/script
- Replace your user group with #. HINT: use the pwd command

STAGE 3 | Log Rotate

More Info: man logrotate

To prevent logs from becoming too large and eventually taking up all of a server's disk space, logs must be rotated. Rotating will take old logs that meet set rules and compress them. A new fresh log will be initiated. When a new threshold is attained, the old compressed logs which have been saved will be deleted. Usually, a log is rotated daily and compressed logs are kept for 7 days.

Create a configuration file to handle log rotation. The configuration file should be named 'logrotate.conf' and should be located within your home directory. Use the following rules for your logrotate configuration:

- Up to a maximum of 6 log files should be rotated
- Logs are to be rotated daily (unless forced more frequently)
- The Log files older than one full cycle are compressed.
- Empty files are subject to log rotation
- The post rotate command is used to recreate the original log fil
- You must rotate both Server_lnfo.log and Server-Hourly.l

STAGE 4 | SSH Keys (server Side)

Perform the following functions on the computer into which you want to log into.

1. Create a '.ssh' directory inside your home directory (It may already exist)
2. Change the permissions of the '.ssh' directory to be rwx------ (Hint: You should use numerical values to set the permissions)
3. Create (by using the touch command) an empty file in the '.ssh' directory called 'authorized_keys'.

The 'authorized_keys' file is a known file by ssh. This means that ssh will look for this file in your home directory when you are connecting to the environment. This file must be named as-is. Any name differences and ssh will not know what it is thus ignoring the file.

STAGE 5 | SSH Keys (Client Side)

For this stage, we will use the SSH server.

4. SSH into the client side using a newly opened terminal

We will now run a script called 'ssh-keygen'. This will generate both a public and private key. When prompted with "Enter file in which to save the key", leave it blank (just press the 'Enter' key). Do the same when it prompts you to enter a passphrase.

Before running the ssh-keygen' command, should always check to make sure that you will run the legitimate version of the command. You don't want to run a rogue version because this may lead to someone stealing your credentials. To check which 'ssh-keygen' command you wilt run, we will use the 'which' command. This command will echo out the full directory path to the command that the system will run.

5. Run the 'which' command as follows

```
$ which ssh-keygen
```

The above command should echo out the following directory path:

/usr/bin/ssh-keygen

If it does not echo out the above directory path, let Josh know immediately.

6. Once we confirm that we are running the legitimate 'ssh-keygen'command, run the command as follows

```
$ ssh-keygen
```

Everything to the right of the I (pipe) is how you would run a command on a remote server. This will ssh into the remote server, execute the command, and return you to the environment you were originally in. Wrapping the command to run in quotes is not required but it is recommended. This is because when you want to run multiple items at once, you will need to wrap them in quotes. Otherwise, the first command will run on the remote server white any other following commands will run on your original server.

.

STAGE 6 | Executing Remote Commands With SSH Keys

With SSH keys, we can execute a remote command without the need to enter a password. It will instead use your SSH key to authenticate.

LAB TWELVE

INTRODUCTION TO JAVASCRIPT I MORE HTML & CSS

The last part of creating a website is making it interactive. This will allow people to interact with your website in real-time without the need to refresh a web page. A popular language to accomplish this is Javascript. In this lab, you will work more with HTML & CSS, but, you will also be adding a hint of Javascript to your web page.

In this lab you will:

- Learn about Javascript

HOW DOES THIS HELP ME WITH MY CAREER

If you go off to work at a job whose primary focus is web applications, or if you go work at a job that maintains their website in-house, you will need to know the basics of the language they use. This way, it will be easier for you to debug what is happening when something isn't quite working once you deploy the application or any of its changes onto your infrastructure. HTML, CSS, and Javascript will always be included in any web page or web application you come across so knowing HTML, CSS, and Javascript is always a must.

You can also be the one who is doing the development work on a web application or a website in which case knowing HTML, CSS, and Javascript is still a must since you will use it no matter what. HTML & CSS are the building blocks to any website and web application, even complicated ones like Facebook while Javascript is the final piece to make a website more appealing to a user by allowing them to interact with it.

STAGE 1| HTML

Let's start things off by setting up our HTML document. To do this, simply type out all the necessary HTML tags. Remember that all of your web pages must be saved inside of your "public-html" directory so be sure to change directories to this directory before continuing. Once you are inside of your "public-html" directory, create a new page called "Emotions.html" and add the following code inside it:

```
< ! DOCTYPE html >

<head>

   < title>Emotions</titıe>

< / head>

<body>

</body>

< / html >
```

Now let's go ahead and add in 3 <div>tags. In between your opening and closing   tags, create the following 3 DIV tags:

- <div id="header"></div>
- <div id="content"></div>
- <div id="footer"></div>

Next we want to create a heading for our webpage. Within the "header" ID'ed DIV tag, add an tag. Within your hl tag, write the following header: "My Current Emotion". It should look like the following:

```
<div id="header">
      <h1>My Current Emotion</hl>
</div>
```

Next, go onto Google Images and search for a happy face image. This can be anything from a smiling cat to an emoji. The image just has to portray a happy feeling. Once you find an image, right-click on the image and copy the image address.

Within your "content" ID\ed DIV tag, add in an image tag. Set the ID of the image to "emotional-face". Paste your image URL within the quotes for 'src'. It should look similar to the following:

```
<div id="content">
        <img id="emotional face" src="paste
image _url here" / >
</div>
```

And finally, within your "footer" ID'ed DIV tag, add a <p> tag. Within the paragraph tag add the following: "This web page is very emotional. Just click on the face to change the way it feels. Don't worry, it doesn't bite...l think :)" It should look similar to the example on the next page.

```
<div id="footer">
    <p>
            This web page is very emotional. Just
            click on the face to change the way it feels.
            Don't worry, it doesn't bite. . .1 think :)

    </p>
</div>
```

Ok, we are now done with our page skeleton. Go ahead and save this webpage. Then open up a web browser and go to the following URL. Remember to change "your-uid" with your actual uid (ex. jsl 234):

> http: / / cit 160 lab . sandbox. csun. edu/ ~ your uid/Emotions . html

Our page looks pretty boring for now. Let's go ahead and style it up a bit using some Embedded CSS.

STAGE 2 | CSS

Let's go back to editing our Emotions. h tml web page so that we can add some sass to this page. We are going to be adding in some embedded CSS. Remember that embedded CSS is CSS that is located on the same web page within the <head> tag. Start off by creating a `<style>`tag within the head tag as shown below:

```
<head>
      < title>Emotions</tit1e>
      < style type="text/css">

      </style>
< / head>
```

Next, we want to change the color of the background to a space grey background. To do this we will change the color of the tag within our CSS. We are going to use color code #474A51. Your code should look like so:

```
< style type="text/css">

body {
background-colour: #474A51;
      }

</style>
```

This is going to make our text a bit unreadable. What we want to do now is change all the text to an off-white color.

We will use #F2F2F2 for the text color. Modify your CSS to do this. It should look like the following:

```
< style
type="
text/cs
s">

     body {

          background-color:
                #474A51;

          color: #F2F2F2;

          }

</style
>
```

Alright, now let's modify the header of the page. Let's change the header to a happy color since we have a happy image. A happy color is usually an off yellow so let's use the hex color #FFFF99. We will need to modify the <hl> HTML tag so we will need to create a new CSS block. Let's also set the font size of the <hl> tag to 21 pixels. Your CSS should now look like the following:

```
<style
type="
text/cs
s">
body {
background—color : #474A51;
color: #F2F2F2;
        )
h1 {
 color:
#FFFF
99;
font-
size:
21px;
</styl
e>
```

Now let's change the size of the image. We are going to change it to a size of 75 x 75. Remember the ID we used with the image tag? We ID'ed the *<img>* tag with "emotional-face". We are going to use this ID when creating our CSS block so that it only affects this image (even though we only have one image). ID's can be useful when you have multiple images and only want to modify 1 image. To apply

CSS to an ID'ed tag, we will type the name of the ID instead of typing in the HTML tag name. We also need to preseed the name with a # symbol. In this case, it will be "#emotional-face". Alright, let's create a new CSS block. Your CSS should now look like the following:

```
<style
type="
text/cs
s">
body {
backgr
ound—
color:
#474A
51;
color:
#F2F2
F2;
}
h1 {
```

```
color:
#FFFF
99;
font-
size:
21px;
}
#emot
ional_
face {
height:
75px;
width:
75px;
)
</styl
e>
```

Alright, that's about it. Let's save our webpage, open up our browser, and browse to our newly updated Emotions , html page.

We're almost done with our page. For our last trick, we will add in some Javascript so that the image can change each time someone clicks on it. We'll also change the color of the <hl> tag to match the new emotion.

STAGE 3 | Javascript

Alright, let's make this a bit more challenging. For this stage of the lab, you will be adding the Javascript code on your own. Add in some Javascript that will do the following:

- When a person clicks on your happy image, change the image to a sad face. Also, change the color of your <h1>HTML tag to E90FF.
- When a person clicks on your sad image, change the image back to your happy image. Also, change the color of your <hl> HTML tag back to its original color.

Some tips for your journey into coding:

- Remember that we ID'ed the image tag "emotional-faces". Use this ID in your Javascript to change the image.
- Create an ID for the <hl> HTML tag. Name it whatever you like. Use this ID in your Javascript to change the color.

- You will need to use an "on click" handler with your Javascript code. This is what will "listen" into when a user clicks on your image.
- Your Javascript code will be written inside of the <head> HTML tags right after the CSS style block, Your Javascript code needs to be inside of a *<script>*HTML tag as shown below:

```
<head>
<style type="text/css">
            # CSS Code Here
      </style>

      <script type="text/javascript">
            # Javascript Code Here
      </script>
</head>
```

LAB THIRTEEN

CONTENT/MIME TYPES I HEADERS I INTRODUCTION TO CGI

We will use a typical real-life tree schema of the Linux shared hosting Control panel to see how the server (Linux) is able to understand the MIME type of a resource requested.

As a result of the browser not being able to understand BASH scripting directly, the CGI allows the web server to process a bash script and then feed the result back to the client.

Above is what a typical web server looks like. In a situation where we are trying to host our web development project, our files are being stored and processed in the "public_html" directory. When we navigate there you can see there's a cgi-bin folder there which also has its part to play in rendering the right MIME-type for a requested resource.

Its permission is set to 755, meaning:

- Owner: Read, Write, Execute
- Group: Read, Execute
- World: Read, Execute

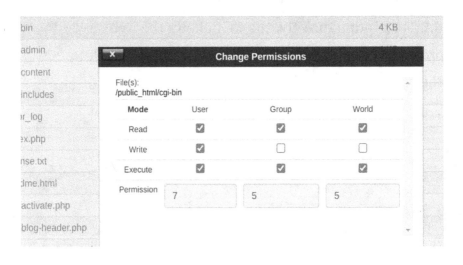

The following are some of the MIME types

For image

- image/* ⇒ represents accepting or serving all kinds of images
- image/apng ⇒ animated portable network graphics (APNG)
- image/avif: AV1 image file format (AVIF)
- image/gif ⇒ Graphics interchange format (GIF)
- image/jpeg ⇒ Joint Photographic expert group image (JPEG)
- image/png ⇒ Portable network graphics (PNG)
- image/svg+xml ⇒ Scalable Vector Graphics (SVG)

For Video

Video Type	Extension	MIME Type
Flash	.flv	video/x-flv
MPEG-4	.mp4	video/mp4
iPhone Index	.m3u8	application/x-mpegURL
iPhone Segment	.ts	video/MP2T
3GP Mobile	.3gp	video/3gpp
QuickTime	.mov	video/quicktime
A/V Interleave	.avi	video/x-msvideo
Windows Media	.wmv	video/x-ms-wmv

Check the overall summary of MIMEs on the next page.

Extension	Kind of document	MIME Type
.aac	AAC audio	audio/aac
.abw	AbiWord ⧉ document	application/x-abiword
.arc	Archive document (multiple files embedded)	application/x-freearc
.avif	AVIF image	image/avif
.avi	AVI: Audio Video Interleave	video/x-msvideo
.azw	Amazon Kindle eBook format	application/vnd.amazon.ebook
.bin	Any kind of binary data	application/octet-stream
.bmp	Windows OS/2 Bitmap Graphics	image/bmp
.bz	BZip archive	application/x-bzip
.bz2	BZip2 archive	application/x-bzip2
.cda	CD audio	application/x-cdf
.csh	C-Shell script	application/x-csh
.css	Cascading Style Sheets (CSS)	text/css
.csv	Comma-separated values (CSV)	text/csv
.doc	Microsoft Word	application/msword
.docx	Microsoft Word (OpenXML)	application/vnd.openxmlformats-officedocument.wordprocessingml.document

`.eot`	MS Embedded OpenType fonts	`application/vnd.ms-fontobject`
`.epub`	Electronic publication (EPUB)	`application/epub+zip`
`.gz`	GZip Compressed Archive	`application/gzip`
`.gif`	Graphics Interchange Format (GIF)	`image/gif`
`.htm` `.html`	HyperText Markup Language (HTML)	`text/html`
`.ico`	Icon format	`image/vnd.microsoft.icon`
`.ics`	iCalendar format	`text/calendar`

`.jar`	Java Archive (JAR)	`application/java-archive`
`.jpeg` `.jpg`	JPEG images	`image/jpeg`
`.js`	JavaScript	`text/javascript` (Specifications: <u>HTML</u> ☐ and <u>RFC 9239</u> ☐)
`.json`	JSON format	`application/json`
`.jsonld`	JSON-LD format	`application/ld+json`
`.mid` `.midi`	Musical Instrument Digital Interface (MIDI)	`audio/midi` `audio/x-midi`
`.mjs`	JavaScript module	`text/javascript`
`.mp3`	MP3 audio	`audio/mpeg`
`.mp4`	MP4 video	`video/mp4`

.mpeg	MPEG Video	`video/mpeg`
.mpkg	Apple Installer Package	`application/vnd.apple.installer+xml`
.odp	OpenDocument presentation document	`application/vnd.oasis.opendocument.presentation`
.ods	OpenDocument spreadsheet document	`application/vnd.oasis.opendocument.spreadsheet`
.odt	OpenDocument text document	`application/vnd.oasis.opendocument.text`
.oga	OGG audio	`audio/ogg`
.ogv	OGG video	`video/ogg`
.ogx	OGG	`application/ogg`
.opus	Opus audio	`audio/opus`
.otf	OpenType font	`font/otf`

`.wav`	Waveform Audio Format	`audio/wav`
`.weba`	WEBM audio	`audio/webm`
`.webm`	WEBM video	`video/webm`
`.webp`	WEBP image	`image/webp`
`.woff`	Web Open Font Format (WOFF)	`font/woff`
`.woff2`	Web Open Font Format (WOFF)	`font/woff2`
`.xhtml`	XHTML	`application/xhtml+xml`
`.xls`	Microsoft Excel	`application/vnd.ms-excel`
`.xlsx`	Microsoft Excel (OpenXML)	`application/vnd.openxmlformats-officedocument.spreadsheetml.sheet`
		`application/xml` is recommended as of RFC 7303 ☑ (section 4.1), but `text/xml` is still used sometimes. You can assign a specific MIME type to a file with `.xml` extension depending on

To see all, visit

https://developer.mozilla.org/en-US/docs/Web/HTTP/Basics_of_HTTP/MIME_types/Common_types

www.ingramcontent.com/pod-product-compliance
Lightning Source LLC
La Vergne TN
LVHW051652050326
832903LV00032B/3760